ANIMAL PLANET™

Sugar Gliders

DAVID E. BORUCHOWITZ

Sugar Gliders

Project Team
Editor: Thomas Mazorlig
Copy Editor:
Indexer:
Design Concept: Leah Lococo Ltd.
Stephanie Krautheim
Design Layout: Mary Ann Kahn

TFH Publications®
President/CEO: Glen S. Axelrod
Executive Vice President: Mark E. Johnson
Publisher: Christopher T. Reggio
Production Manager: Kathy Bontz

TFH Publications, Inc.®
One TFH Plaza
Third and Union Avenues
Neptune City, NJ 07753

Printed and bound in China.
11 12 13 14 15   1 3 5 7 9 8 6 4 2

Library of Congress Cataloging-in-Publication Data
Boruchowitz, David E.
  Sugar gliders / David E. Boruchowitz.
     p. cm.
  Includes index.
  ISBN 978-0-7938-3711-3 (alk. paper)
  1. Sugar gliders as pets. 2. Sugar glider. I. Title.
  SF459.S83B67 2012
  636.935'83--dc23

                         2011049947

This book has been published with the intent to provide accurate and authoritative information in regard to the subject matter within. While every reasonable precaution has been taken in preparation of this book, the author and publisher expressly disclaim responsibility for any errors, omissions, or adverse effects arising from the use or application of the information contained herein. The techniques and suggestions are used at the reader's discretion and are not to be considered a substitute for veterinary care. If you suspect a medical problem consult your veterinarian.

Note: In the interest of concise writing, "he" is used when referring to puppies and dogs unless the text is specifically referring to females or males. "She" is used when referring to people. However, the information contained herein is equally applicable to both sexes.

The Leader in Responsible Animal Care for Over 50 Years!®

www.tfh.com

Table of Contents

Chapter 1

Why I Adore My

Sugar Glider

What's soft, furry, friendly, and loves to ride around in your pocket? There are quite a few pets that might fit that description, but if we add "has big eyes and carries its babies in a pouch like a kangaroo," the only answer would be: a sugar glider!

The sugar glider is known to scientists as *Petaurus breviceps*, which means roughly "short-headed rope walker," a reference to the ease with which the animal negotiates through the tangle of tiny branches and twigs high in its forest habitat home. However, this animal is much more agile and acrobatic than the nimblest human tightrope artist.

At first glance, a sugar glider looks like a rodent—a squirrel or a flying squirrel. You'd never guess that he was a relative of koalas and kangaroos, or even of the common opossum! Yet a sugar glider is in fact a marsupial from Australasia (Australia, New Guinea, and surrounding islands).

Perfect Pocket Pets?

Pocket pets describe any of the small mammals often kept as pets, including hamsters, gerbils, mice, rats, and guinea pigs. Sugar gliders are also considered pocket pets. These small mammals with plush, soft fur are not as common as hamsters or gerbils, but they are becoming more and more popular all the time—and for good reason! In fact, a glider might just be the perfect pet for you. This book will provide all the details to help you decide if it is. It is very important that you understand that gliders are not like mice, rats, hamsters, gerbils, and other pocket pets. These very special, cuddly animals from the other side of

Sugar gliders are tree-dwelling animals found in Australia, New Guinea, and many of the surrounding islands.

the world have very special needs and provide very special rewards. Before we look at what a sugar glider is, let's consider what a sugar glider isn't.

A Sugar Glider Is Not a Rodent

Although they could easily be mistaken for rodents, sugar gliders are not rodents. There are close to 10,000 species of rodents in the world, and they are found in just about every habitat. Many are considered vermin, and many have spread across the globe with the human population. Since rodents encompass so many species, exceptions always exist, but generally rodents are small, secretive, and omnivorous. They are characterized by short gestation periods, rapid growth and maturity, significant fecundity, and short lifespans. For example, hamster babies are born 16 days after the parents mate, and the young can be ready to mate less than two months after birth. The number of babies in a single litter is usually about eight but can be up to 20. A female may have five or more litters per year. If all the offspring lived, a single female hamster could have thousands of descendants within a year. A hamster's lifespan is only a couple of years or so.

Such rapid growth and reproduction is typical of rodents. Baby hamsters are born naked, blind, and helpless; but in a few days, they have fur, and at a week they begin to walk around, explore, and even eat solid food. Their eyes open at two weeks of age, and they are weaned in another week or two.

FAMILY-FRIENDLY TIP

Are Sugar Gliders for Your Child?

The concept of a "pocket pet" typically brings to mind mice, rats, hamsters, and gerbils. These rodents can make excellent companions for a responsible young person and will, in fact, enjoy riding around in the child's pocket. While sugar gliders are perhaps the perfect pocket pets in this respect and will gladly snuggle in a pocket all day, young children should not be trusted with their care and handling.

In fact, given its long lifespan and its habit of deeply bonding with its owner, a sugar glider is perhaps a better pet for an adult. It may be best for the parents of a young child to adopt a glider as a pet and let the child "help" take care of him. The child can assume progressively more responsibility over the years and wind up with a faithful friend that will accompany her right into young adulthood.

So, What Is a Sugar Glider?

Sugar gliders, too, are small, secretive, and omnivorous, but because they are marsupials (which we'll discuss in a moment), their growth and reproduction is quite slow, and they have a lifespan much more like that of a dog or a cat—about 15 years.

Glider litters are small—usually producing only one or two babies, although there can be up to four—and the young take a long time to grow, not venturing from the nest until they are about four months old. There is some variation, but sexual maturity is reached usually between six and eighteen months of age. In the wild, a female will have two or three litters per year. A single female glider typically has fewer than a dozen descendants in a year. Thus, despite many similarities to rodents, sugar gliders are markedly different in their life cycles.

Other common names for these adorable animals are flying possum, flying phalanger, honey glider, lesser flying phalanger, short-headed flying phalanger, and squirrel glider. The name "phalanger," which is applied to the sugar glider and many of its close relatives, refers to their long fingers (phalanges). But, why all those "flying" names?

Flying Squirrels?

Bats are the only mammals that can actually fly, but several species of flying squirrels and flying phalangers can glide gracefully from tree to tree.

Pet sugar gliders can live for up to 15 years, much longer than their wild counterparts.

A Long-Time Friend

In the wild, a nine-year-old sugar glider would be considered old, but that is because the rigors of life in the forest favor the young. In captivity, sugar gliders can live from 12 to 15 years, meaning that they are as long-lived as many dogs and cats. There are even reports of female sugar gliders more than 10 years old successfully raising a litter of joeys. When you bring a glider into your home, it is the beginning of a very long relationship.

These animals have large flaps of skin that are normally held folded against the body. When the creature wants to move to another tree to find food or to escape a predator, he spreads these skin flaps by holding his arms and legs straight out from his body, thus stretching the skin, which is attached to his fingers and toes; then he jumps out into midair. Like a parachute, the skin slows the animal's descent, and he can angle one way or the other to steer toward his goal of a distant tree. The sugar glider also uses his tail as a rudder. As he approaches his target, he makes a short upward glide and lands on a tree trunk or branch with all four feet at once. Obviously, the higher the animal is when he jumps, the farther he can glide without ending up on the ground.

Since many of the common predators of the sugar glider—carnivorous mammals and reptiles—cannot fly, being able to glide up to 300 feet (100 meters) or more is a very useful defense! It can sometimes work even against birds of prey, like owls, since if the glider jumps after the bird dives, the bird may not be able to redirect its attack in time.

The similarities between the flying squirrel (a rodent) and the sugar glider (a marsupial) are quite astounding. Biologists refer to cases like this as convergence, in which unrelated animals in similar ecological niches share many traits that were independently developed, rather than inherited from a common ancestor.

O, Possum!

Although in the United States a possum is the same thing as an opossum, elsewhere a distinction is often made between "opossums" of the family Didelphidae (the group of Western-Hemisphere marsupials that includes the Virginia opossum) and the only distantly related "possums" of the superfamily Phalangeroidea (the group of Eastern-Hemisphere marsupials that includes the sugar glider).

Sugar gliders are nocturnal animals, and their large eyes and ears enable them to find food and avoid danger in the dark.

Form and Function

Both flying squirrels and sugar gliders have big eyes and small, light bodies with long furry tails and gliding membranes stretched from hands to feet. They climb, jump, and glide in very similar ways, using their very similar body structures. They also have a similar coloration of dark stripes along a brownish grey body, which they share that with a host of other small mammals. Such coloration offers effective camouflage for their secretive, hide-as-defense lifestyles.

Behavior and Lifestyle

Spending most of their life high in treetops, foraging at night among the branches and nesting in hollows during the day, both sugar gliders and flying squirrels share similar habits. Some of the foods they eat are the same, but the rodents need a more grain- and nut-based diet, while the gliders need more fruits and meat.

Mammals with Pouches

The marsupials are pouched mammals found mostly in Australia and nearby Asian islands, although there are several species in South America and one in North America. Female marsupials have a marsupium—a pouch or fur-lined pocket in which her nipples are located and which has a slit opening. Koala bears and kangaroos are probably the most well known marsupials, but there are many, many types of marsupials. Although they have fur and produce milk for their young, they are quite different from other mammals such as cows, cats, gerbils, or people, which are known as placental mammals.

Marsupial Reproduction

The most important difference between the two types of mammals—marsupials and placental—is in the way in which marsupials give birth and nurture their young. Most mammal babies grow in their mother's uterus for a long time, where they are nourished through a complex placenta, an organ that transfers substances from the mother's bloodstream to the baby's, and vice versa. These babies are born at quite a large size and grow quickly.

Marsupials, however, have only a rudimentary placenta-like organ. The babies grow for only a short time inside their mother's uterus and are born at a very tiny size. The only parts of their bodies that are fairly well developed at birth are the front legs and the mouth.

Using their strong front legs, the babies climb over the mother's fur and find the opening to the pouch. Once safe and warm inside, a baby marsupial latches on to one of its mother's nipples and doesn't let go for anything. In fact, if he is removed from the nipple he cannot reattach and will die. The mother's milk nourishes the babies for a long time, during which they finish developing all their body parts and grow large enough to handle life outside the pouch. Even once the babies are able to leave their mother's pouch and begin to learn how to survive in their world, they may return to the pouch to nurse, to sleep, or to hide from danger.

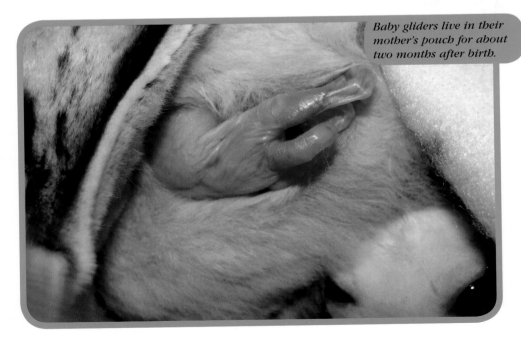

Baby gliders live in their mother's pouch for about two months after birth.

A Word on Exotics

You will often see sugar gliders and many other animals called "exotic pets." The distinction between exotic and non-exotic pets is not always clear, but in most cases it is based on some measurement of domestication. Some species that are kept as companion animals, such as dogs and cats, were domesticated in prehistoric times. In some cases, a domesticated animal is a species unto itself, and you cannot find its ancestral species in the wild—these may include, depending on which authority you follow, dogs, goats, horses, cattle, and society finches. Any such animal kept as a pet is definitely not an exotic. On the other hand, a tame raccoon, kinkajou, or turtle is considered an exotic pet.

One of the most prominent characteristics of domestication is a condition known as neoteny, the biological term for the retention of juvenile characteristics into adulthood. For example, wolf pups bark, but adult wolves almost never do. Many neotenous traits are behavioral, and the typical tractability and tameness of domestic animals often contrast greatly with the behavior of their wild counterparts, in the same way that wild animal young are often safe to have around while the adults are definitely not. The charge often leveled against exotic pets is that, when they mature, their instincts win out over their socialization to people.

In fact, domestication is often viewed as a process of selectively breeding out many instinctive behaviors. While biologically a gross oversimplification, it is true that wild animals possess instincts that their domesticated cousins do not, instincts that create problems when they are kept as companion animals. It is relatively easy to get a dog to accept you as alpha, and the animal remains tractable his whole life. A wolf, on the other hand, no matter how tame he is and no matter how affectionate he is, will always, every minute of every day, be looking for ways to challenge your alpha status and to move up in the hierarchy of its pack. Since its pack is your family, this can be a dangerous situation.

It is not a situation of instinct winning out over socialization, but of socialization instincts at work! To a wolf, there are two types of wolves: pack members and outsiders. Outsiders need to be driven off, violently if necessary. Within the pack, there are two types of wolves: alphas and underlings. When you socialize a wolf pup to human beings, he accepts them as his pack. He will viciously protect

your family from other people, making him a fantastic guard animal—but he will also challenge your alpha status whenever he perceives you as weak or inattentive. That is simply the way of life in a wolf pack.

Well, what about sugar gliders? You could say that they are making the transition from exotic to domesticated with each successive generation born in captivity, but they are still exotic pets—essentially tamed wild animals. They do retain their wild instincts, but they are not herd animals or predators, and their instincts do not make them dangerous to be around. In fact, the deep emotional bonding that is the foundation of a glider colony is what makes them such interactive and endearing companions. It is likely that gliders view humans as the lowest in the dominance hierarchy of their colony. After all, we don't share the nest, scent mark the other gliders, or participate in the tussles and games that certainly figure into these matters. We never even climb the drapes, not to mention never gliding anywhere!

Challenging the alpha isn't really part of a glider's behavior in the first place, but a human probably always would fail such a challenge, simply by not recognizing it in the first place and by failing to respond correctly.

Two Types of Mammals

Marsupials and placental mammals share many features but also differ greatly.
Here is a summary of some of their shared and unique traits.

Trait	Marsupials	Placental Mammals
Fur/Hair	Yes	Yes
Give birth	Yes	Yes
Produce milk	Yes	Yes
Pregnancy	Very short	Long
Babies at birth	Barely developed	Well-developed
Babies after birth	Long time in pouch	In nest or travel with parent(s)
General anatomy	Many differences from humans	Basically the same as humans

Sugar Glider Specifics

Having large babies in her pouch is certainly an aerodynamic problem, so sugar glider joeys (the name for the babies while in the pouch) leave the pouch earlier than many other marsupials and are cared for in a nest by the male and any other members of the colony while the mother is out foraging.

Like hamsters, sugar gliders are born after a pregnancy of only 16 days, but they are nowhere near as developed as newborn hamsters, and they still have to spend about two months growing in their mother's pouch (at which age hamster babies are already off on their own, starting their own families). When gliders leave their mother's pouch, they are just starting to get fur and their eyes are still closed. They spend another two months in the nest, cared for by all the adults in the group, until they finally venture out into the world.

It is always best to have more than one pet glider because they are extremely social animals.

Marsupial Diversity

Although marsupials once lived all around the world, today almost all of them are found in or near Australia. Until Europeans arrived in Australia with their rats, cats, and livestock, the only placental mammals on the continent were human beings and dingoes, dogs brought by the ancestors of the Aborigines. In the absence of placental mammals, marsupials filled every ecological niche; there are rodent-like marsupials, carnivore-type marsupials, and odd animals like kangaroos and wombats that fill the ecological role of hoofed animals elsewhere.

Among the rodent-like marsupials are the squirrel-like marsupials, which include those we are interested in here: the flying-squirrel-like marsupials known as sugar gliders. They are extremely successful animals and continue to thrive despite loss of habitat to human development. They have become popular pets in many places far from their native lands. In the rest of this book, we will take a detailed look at these fascinating creatures and explain their proper care so that you can decide if you might enjoy sharing your life with them.

Can You Keep One Glider?

Gliders are naturally social animals and live together in groups of about half a dozen to a dozen animals, although they are occasionally found in groups of 50 individuals. They are almost never alone. The colony feeds, sleeps, and moves together, and they raise the babies together.

Many people believe that you should never get just one glider, and even those who say that you can keep just one if you provide very special conditions for him agree that it is always better to have at least two. This is because of the enormous time demands on the owner of a single sugar glider.

Time Commitment

Sugar gliders require a considerable time commitment both in terms of their daily care and in terms of bonding and other social needs. One of the time demands is food preparation. The unusual dietary requirements of these animals have so far prevented the creation of a boxed or canned diet that meets all of their needs, so fresh

How Many Gliders?

It is extremely difficult—almost impossible—to keep one sugar glider. They are such social animals that a lone glider often will not survive. Many breeders will not sell just one glider. You should get at least two so that they can keep each other company when you are not able to be with them.

food must be prepared for them every evening. For the most part, the only difference between preparing a single glider's dinner and making food for a group of gliders is in the quantities involved—it doesn't take any longer to mix up a double or triple batch. Some of the food can be frozen into single-serving portions (an ice cube tray makes this simple) and thawed for daily use. Fresh fruits and vegetables can be added to the thawed mixture.

Bonding, playing, and interacting are the other major time demands, and in this case, the more gliders you have, the smaller the demand on you. While you sleep, your group of gliders will entertain each other, keeping each other company, playing together, and staying healthy and happy without your input. You must still give them daily attention and affection to keep them bonded to you, to keep them considering you as part of their group, but you do not need to be the group, as you must with a single glider.

Keeping One

A single sugar glider in a cage is a miserable creature, and he may get so depressed that he dies. For a lone glider to thrive, you will have to take the place of his group. This requires a lot of commitment on your part. Some experts say that a minimum of four hours per day interacting with your pet is required, while others believe this isn't anywhere near enough. Since a glider can live for 15 years, this is a large responsibility. Basically, a single sugar glider needs to be your almost-

It is best to start with a pair or group of gliders that are already bonded to each other.

constant companion. Since a glider is active from dusk to dawn, your companionship will be most important during that period, and watching you sleep does not in any way count as social activity for a sugar glider.

People who keep single glider pets are . . . well, extremely dedicated to say the least. For example, some owners make and wear pouches—special sacks that the animal can rest in without scratching their human companion's skin. These pouches allow them to take their pet to work with them in their pocket. Basically, they become a surrogate sugar glider

and spend almost all of their time with the animal.

You are undoubtedly considering sugar gliders as pets that you will enjoy spending time with, but not as constant companions. Therefore, in this book, we will assume that you will be keeping two or more gliders. If you decide you want only one, you must remember that the care described in this book is absolutely not sufficient for a single glider, and you must find out from the rare breeder who is willing to sell you just one animal how to take care of him.

Legalities

Keeping More than One

On the other hand, if you keep more than one sugar glider, they will keep each other company. In this case, you still need to spend a lot of time with them so that they will remain bonded to you. They won't require this for their own happiness, but it is vital if they are to stay cuddly pocket pets. Without sufficient human interaction, gliders can become very shy and afraid of being handled. Plus, the more they accept you as a member of their group, the more relaxed they'll be with you, and the more fun you'll have playing with them.

Starting Together

Even though sugar gliders are social, they do not take well to strangers. In the wild, a colony lives together all the time, defending their small territory against other gliders. There, a skirmish normally leads to the hasty retreat of the invaders—but in the confines of a cage, it often becomes a fight to the death. Whatever combination of gliders you want to have, it should be put together right from the start. When baby gliders are raised together in the same household, sharing their cage, nest, and food with each other, they will remain a happy group. If you try to add a new animal to the group, it will usually end in tragedy. A sugar glider can and will occasionally kill another sugar glider.

In special cases, it is possible to get adult gliders to accept each other, especially in the case when one member of a pair dies. The remaining animal is often so despondent that he will appreciate the company of a new animal, and the two will bond. The best way to begin is to house the animals in adjoining cages, allowing them to have a little time together once they show signs of accepting each other through the wire. If that goes well, their time together can be increased gradually until it is safe to leave them together all the time. Whenever the bonding of strangers is attempted, the owner must keep a very close eye on things and be ready to intervene if any aggression arises.

Basic Anatomy

As one of the smallest marsupials, the adult sugar glider's body is about 6 to 8 inches (15 to 20 cm) long, and his long, furry tail adds another 6 to 8 inches (15 to 20 cm) or so. His weight is between 4 and 6 ounces (115 and 170 g). The males are at the larger end of this spectrum, and the females at the smaller end.

Several anatomical features of the sugar glider are especially notable.

Patagium

The first is clearly the patagium, the flap of skin used for gliding. It is thin, furred, and flexible, stretching from the hand to the foot. Normally, it is folded up against the body and hardly visible. When the animal leaps, he spreads out his four legs, pulling the patagium taut and creating the airfoil that enables him to soar from one tree to another over considerable distances. By changing the shape of the patagium, the glider is able to alter his course, steering to a specific target. At the end of the glide, he does a quick upturn and lands on the trunk or branch on all fours.

Hands and Feet

Like humans, sugar gliders have five digits on each hand and foot, but they also have a thumb on their feet! This large, opposable first toe is used to help hang on to branches. The next two toes are *syndactylous*, meaning they are fused into one. This unusual digit is used for grooming and is also thought to be an adaptation for climbing.

Scent Glands

Sugar gliders have an acute sense of smell, and their social organization is largely based on odor. They mark their territories and each other with their scent glands. Adults of both sexes have numerous scent glands, but males have more prominent scent glands, including one on the head (the "bald spot") and one on the chest.

Humans can detect the mild odor, and most people do not find it offensive. Male gliders who have been neutered do not develop the large scent glands, and if they are neutered after maturity, their scent glands atrophy.

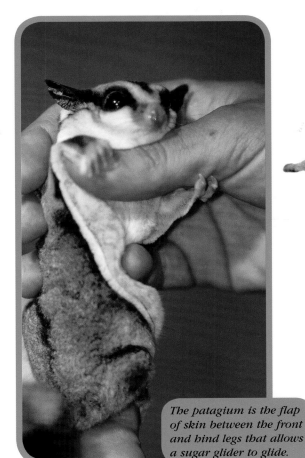

The patagium is the flap of skin between the front and hind legs that allows a sugar glider to glide.

Male or Female?

Although some people claim one sex of glider makes a better pet than the other, they don't agree on which that is. Gliders of either sex will get along if raised together, but you do not want to get a male and a female unless the male is neutered. Breeding gliders is very different from keeping gliders, and it is something properly left to licensed professionals. So get two gliders of the same sex, or make sure the male is neutered. While neutering males is a simple operation, the spaying of female gliders is not easily performed and is generally not recommended by veterinarians.

In fact, it is best only to keep neutered males, even if you don't have a female. Intact males can present problems with aggression and scent marking, all of which neutering prevents.

Fur

The fur of a sugar glider is thick, velvety, and plush. The little animals spend a lot of time grooming themselves and each other, and they usually keep their fur neat and clean. Dominant males may get a bit of oily discoloration around their scent glands, especially on the chest, but that is normal. A healthy pelt is the sign of a healthy glider, and if your pet develops thin fur or bare patches, take him quickly to the vet.

Eyes

One place a sugar glider really differs from most rodents is in the eyes. The glider's eyes are more lemur-like than rodent-like, being large and positioned on the front of the face. Being nocturnal, the flying squirrel also benefits from larger-than-usual rodent eyes, but these are positioned on the sides of his head, rather than facing straight forward as the glider's do. In fact, the glider's big, soulful eyes are a major source of appeal, and along with his facial markings and tiny pink nose, are certain to produce claims of "So cute!" among his human friends.

Ears

The dark, floppy ears of a glider do a lot more than add to his appeal. As a small animal in a dark forest full of predators, a glider needs acute hearing to help him keep in touch with his environment. In addition, gliders communicate using a variety of sounds, and they use their barking to alert other members of the colony who might be out of sight.

Tail

The furry tail of a sugar glider acts as a rudder when he is gliding. It also assists in balance while the animal scampers around the treetops. The tail is also somewhat prehensile; a glider may use it to carry nesting materials back to the nest.

Voice

Sugar gliders are surprisingly vocal. They produce a variety of sounds to communicate with each other—and with you! The two most significant sounds are called *barking and crabbing.*

Barking is exactly that—a yelp that may be repeated many times. It normally communicates excitement of some type, often alarm. Gliders also bark when they are out of sight of each other, and they will bark to say "Get in here!" to you. Their habit of barking at night makes a bedroom a bad choice of location for their cage.

Crabbing is a grouchy sound, sometimes likened to the sound of an electric pencil sharpener. It expresses displeasure and may be used when you

Male gliders have a scent gland on their head that makes them look like they have a bald spot.

Many Colors

While many species are called sugar gliders, only one is common in the pet trade. There are, however, several different color variations of that animal, and it is likely that, as time goes on and more and more generations are raised in captivity, even more new colors will appear. The normal wild-type glider is the most common, but several color changes have occurred in captivity. Some of these are well understood and have been fixed into true-breeding strains. For others, the genetics is not understood yet, and breeders are working to figure things out. Unfortunately, many of the "experts" on glider genetics demonstrate considerable misunderstanding of basic genetic principles, so you should treat anything you hear or read on the subject as tentative. Several strains of gliders have problems with male sterility, although other strains of the same color do not.

All colors of sugar gliders make equally wonderful companions. Sugar glider coloration also varies due to environmental rather than genetic differences. The animals' usual scent marking can affect the fur's color. Diet is also a factor, as is age. The elusive "red series" glider colorations are thought by some to come and go at various stages of life.

Keep in mind that, in addition to a misunderstanding of genetics, different people may use different names for the same color, or even the same name for different colors. Also, different colors and combinations of colors may be very difficult to tell apart by looking at the animals. Sugar gliders in the more common colors are not much more expensive than regular wild-type gliders, but some of the rarer colors bring extremely high prices—in the many thousands of dollars. For pets, the only significant thing is that you like the way they look; only commercial breeders need to worry about identifying, testing, and tracking all the color types, and even they don't always agree on which is which.

Current colors include:

- Albino
- Blonde
- Buttercream
- Chocolate
- Cinnamon
- Cremino
- Gray
- Leucistic
- Lion
- Platinum
- Red cinnamon
- Ringtail
- White face
- White tip

leucistic

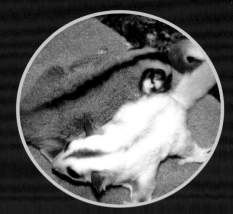

platinum and normal

white-faced blonde

albino

white tip

Sugar gliders bond deeply with their owners and enjoy spending time with—and on—their humans.

disturb a sleeping glider.

Their other vocalizations include various chirps and whistles. Part of the fun in keeping sugar gliders is trying to identify the noises they make and figure out what they are used to convey.

Personality and Behavior

Sugar gliders aren't just cute, cuddly, and friendly; they also are full of personality and will constantly surprise and delight you with the things they do. They will treat you as a friend, a source of treats to be ferreted out (*I just know you've got a mealworm hidden somewhere!*), and a tree—great for climbing on, launching off from, and gliding onto.

Bonding

Sugar gliders bond very deeply with their owners. It is a lifelong relationship for the little marsupials and a meaningful, many-year-long one for their humans. Gliders may look like a mouse or gerbil at first glance, but they entangle themselves in our hearts in the same way a cherished dog or cat might. In addition to that ineffable pet–owner bond that transcends the gap between people and a huge variety of animals, sugar gliders are more than happy to accept you as a member of their troupe, a member of their family. You will feel the same way toward them.

Other Traits

Sugar gliders are energetic, acrobatic, and curious. They play hard and sleep

Small Size, Big Voice

Sugar gliders make many different sounds, ranging from soft chirping to loud barking. Many people are amazed to hear such noise from a small animal. Although a squawking parrot or barking dog is much noisier, a glider's vocalizations will surprise someone expecting only a squirrel-like chattering.

hard, and they greet new challenges with cautious eagerness. They are good at figuring out cage door latches and experts in getting into places that their owners were sure were inaccessible. They are content to snuggle in a pocket for hours while their human wastes perfectly good sleeping time doing other things. They approach life with gusto and meals with enthusiasm. They are small animals with giant hearts, and if you are willing to spend the considerable amount of time sugar gliders demand, they will work their way into your heart in no time.

Chapter 2

The Stuff of
Everyday
Life

Just as you have objects and materials that help enhance your quality of life, your sugar gliders have certain needs that can only be met if you provide the objects and materials they require. Certainly foremost among these is a cage.

A Refuge, not a Prison

Your gliders' cage is a home, not a prison. You will certainly spend a great deal of time playing and just snuggling with your pets, but they need a safe, secure place where they can spend time when you are not interacting with them. Their main nest will be in the cage, so their natural instinct to head home to the nest makes their cage a place of refuge, not confinement.

Keeping in

Whenever you are not keeping an eye on your gliders, they must be secure in their cage. An unattended sugar glider is in great danger. If you have other pets, they could harm or even kill your gliders, or the gliders could kill them. A human household itself presents numerous potential dangers—

everything from whirling fans with lethal blades to toilets that present a drowning hazard.

And, although your gliders may be totally bonded to you and love to stay near you, when you are gone, their natural curiosity and explorative instincts can lead them far astray. Small gaps in woodwork, heating ducts, and other openings can give them access to other rooms, or even to the outside. Be aware that sugar gliders can fit through extremely small openings— under doors, in gaps around pipes, and even down sink drains.

A sugar glider's natural curiosity and playfulness make him a danger to your household possessions as well. Unsupervised gliders may shred your curtains or

Coming Home

When you first bring your gliders home, you should allow them a couple of days in their cage to get used to their new environment. If they are not afraid and do not crab when you reach for them, you can pet them in the cage and offer them a few treats. If they show signs of stress, just leave them alone to settle in for a day or two.

Since very few cages are large enough for people to enter, a bonding tent is often the tool used to get gliders accustomed to their new owners after they have settled in. An actual tent works well, but any makeshift enclosure will do. You can drape a blanket over a couple of chairs and weight the edges with books around the perimeter. Gently pick up a glider and take him with you into the tent. Bring a few treats in your pocket. Then release the animal and let him explore the tent—and you. Let him find the treats if he readily climbs over your clothing; otherwise, offer them to encourage the glider to come close.

Continue to use the tent until your new pets are at ease when being handled by you, which should not take very long if they were properly handled by their breeder.

knock items off shelves. Gliders gnaw on just about anything, and they may decide that there is some tasty sap in the wood of your furniture. If they should chew on an electric cord they could be electrocuted and possibly start a fire.

Keeping out

A cage also serves to keep harmful things out. Cats and dogs can pose a serious threat to gliders, even when the animals get along fine while you are watching them. The natural predatory instinct remains in all cats and dogs to some extent, and sometimes a glider's movement or posture will trigger an attack. A secure cage prevents such a tragedy.

Placement

Small animals mean dinner to larger, meat-eating animals, so in the wild

Place your gliders cage in a quiet area of your home, away from drafts or direct sunlight.

---

sugar gliders must always be on guard against predators. Birds of prey can swoop down and pluck a glider off a branch; snakes, other reptiles, and predatory mammals can sneak up on one in a tree. The only defenses the poor little possum has are to run—or glide—away and to hide. A glider in the open is a glider at risk, and his instincts tell him always to stay safe.

For your pets to feel safe, their cage must be in a quiet spot, preferably not on the floor, since they naturally associate height with safety. If you can manage it, a cage that goes right up to the ceiling will give your gliders a treetop-like view that they will instinctively consider safe and relaxing.

Lights Out

Sugar gliders are naturally nocturnal; they prefer to sleep all day and become active in the evening. This doesn't mean you can't have any interaction with them during the day. Pet gliders love to ride around snuggled in your pocket or in a sleeping pouch.

They also may wake up for something interesting enough, perhaps to sample a treat, but for the most part you should not bother them or try to awaken them during the day.

Avoid placing the cage in a drafty area, or on or near heater or air conditioning vents. A cage put in front of a sunny window can heat up excessively, and the bright light may upset your pets. A cage near a door may be chilly, if not from a draft then whenever the door is opened in cold weather.

Construction

Many types of cages work well for sugar gliders: manufactured and homemade, traditional or innovative. A tall cage is best. Because gliders are climbing animals who spend most of their lives up in trees, they appreciate height much more than floor space. Of course, increased floor space also means more "treetop" space, so a tall and wide cage gives plenty of room at the top for playing and exercise.

Metal Cages

A glider's metal cage should be made of horizontal bars or welded wire, not vertical bars, so the animal can climb freely around it. Galvanized wire should be coated in some way so that the animals cannot lick or chew the zinc coating. Plastic mesh can work, although if it's not thick enough, the gliders may chew through it. You can get the best of both worlds with cages made from vinyl-clad metal mesh, which looks nice and is easy to keep clean. The spacing between wires or bars must be ½-inch (1 cm) or less to prevent injury

or escape. A wire bottom over a litter pan makes cleaning the cage easy.

Acrylic Cages

Because of their similar habits, birds and gliders offer many of the same housing challenges. Probably the biggest challenge is trying to contain the mess that the animals fling about, which creates a perimeter of cleanup around the cage. What's worse, the gooey splatter of gliders is worse than the feathers, seed hulls, and bits of food tossed about by birds. A solution to this problem that also offers superb visibility of your pets is an acrylic cage, one made of transparent plastic panels.

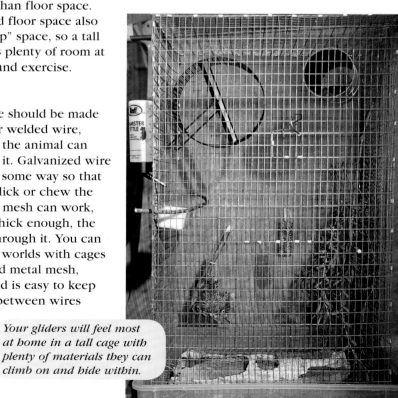

Your gliders will feel most at home in a tall cage with plenty of materials they can climb on and hide within.

The mess will be easily visible on the clear walls of the enclosure, but it will not fly around the room, and it is easily wiped off with a wet rag every morning.

Some acrylic cage designs feature a wire top for ventilation, although some are solid all around and have screened air holes around the sides of the cage. In either case, the occupants are protected from drafts. The flexibility of acrylic is a great advantage. It can easily be formed into a cylinder to provide a no-corners cage.

The only drawback to these cages is the loss of the cage walls as climbing and exercising areas. To compensate, you should use an abundance of branches, ropes, and other climbing features inside the cage. Acrylic is a bit on the expensive side, but it offers great possibilities for your sugar gliders' home.

Size

The minimal size for a cage for your gliders is about 30 to 36 inches (75 to 90 cm) square, and at least 36 inches (90 cm) high. This represents the minimum, and a larger cage is much better. There must be ample room for the gliders to play actively, since much of their most active periods will be while you are asleep and they are confined to their cage.

Many glider owners purchase a large parrot cage. These cages, intended for macaws and Amazons, are big—often 4 to 6 feet (1 to 2 meters) long and high. They are typically made of powder-coated metal strong

Homemade Cages

Although there are a great many commercially available cages that are perfect for sugar gliders, if you're handy, you can certainly make your own. Coated hardware cloth or similar wire mesh is a very suitable material for the glider cage. Wood is not a good choice; gliders may gnaw on it, and it will become soiled.

enough to hold up to an extremely powerful beak. They also have horizontal bars that enable a parrot to climb easily. All of these traits make such a cage ideal for sugar gliders as well. One of the great advantages of such a large cage is that if you are unable to take your gliders out to play for a couple of evenings, they can still get plenty of exercise in their cage. When housed in smaller cages, gliders are much more dependent on outside play time for their proper exercise. The bar spacing on some large bird cages will be too far apart for gliders. Make sure that the bars are narrowly spaced so that your pets will not escape or get injured.

Wire cages provide gliders with a lot of climbing space, along with plenty of places to hang toys.

Nests

Sugar gliders naturally seek cavities in tree trunks and branches as nests. They will readily use a wooden nestbox made for parakeets or lovebirds. Sometimes plastic nestboxes are available, and they are much easier to keep clean. Provide some wood shavings, straw, or dried leaves as nesting material. The only disadvantage to a wooden nestbox is that it will need to be cleaned occasionally. This is best accomplished by scrubbing the box inside and out with a dilute bleach solution (follow label instructions for preparing a

Substrate

The substrate you use in the cage isn't really very important, since gliders rarely spend time on the ground or on the bottom of their cage. When outfitting their home, definitely think of your gliders as if they were birds. The bowls, toys, and nests should all be located up in the cage, hanging on the sides, rather than placed on the cage floor. A sugar glider on the ground instinctively feels exposed and unsafe.

If the cage has a wire base grid over a tray, place newspaper, paper towels, wood shavings, or cat litter in it. There is some concern that cedar and pine shavings may cause respiratory ailments in small animals, so many opt for aspen shavings or litter made from corn cobs. You only need enough substrate to absorb a day's wastes, since it should be changed daily.

FAMILY-FRIENDLY TIP

Helping Hands

The complexities of sugar glider housing, maintenance, feeding, and handling mean that children cannot bear the whole responsibility of caring for the family gliders. Even the youngest, however, can be given tasks—such as holding a food dish or putting new toys into the cage—so they feel part of the process. Older children can be given progressively more responsibilities as they learn and demonstrate understanding of the proper methods of caring for and handling sugar gliders.

disinfecting solution), then air drying it, preferably in direct sunshine. Keep two boxes and rotate them, with a clean, dry one always in reserve.

To facilitate cleanliness, some glider owners opt for fabric nests, hanging one or more sleeping pouches in the cage. Gliders take to these readily, and the pouches are easily laundered when dirty. It is especially important to make sure the fabric will not catch toenails and to check the pouches for any exposed seams that can snare a nail. A glider caught in cloth threads can be injured or killed very quickly. Fleece-like material is the safest to use.

Nests can be made of a number of suitable materials. This one is made from a section of PVC pipe.

Sleeping Pouches

Many people feel that a sugar glider's affinity for sleeping pouches is due to its being a marsupial and having a memory of being in its mother's pouch. Actually, though, he shares this affinity with many other small mammals, all of which share the trait of nesting in cavities or burrows. Whatever the explanation, your sugar gliders will appreciate a variety of slings, pouches, and nests in which they can sleep, either in their cage or on your person.

A sleeping pouch can be as simple and generic as your jacket pocket or as specialized as a custom-made sack.

Many people make their own pouches. The threat from loose threads is much less when the pouch is only used for the glider, when you are carrying him around. Since you will always be there to free a nail before the animal gets hopelessly entangled, there are many more suitable choices for a carrying pouch as opposed to a nest pouch.

Food and Water Bowls

Many hanging bowls and cups made for birds work very well for sugar gliders as well. These are typically made of plastic, glass, stainless steel, or ceramic, which makes cleanup very easy. They should be hung high up in the cage, not set on the floor. Stainless steel bowls are the most durable: they won't shatter if dropped, and gliders can't chew them up.

While you can offer water to your gliders in a bowl, it is much more sanitary to use a water bottle, such as those sold for watering small rodents. Your pets may already be used to using one, but if not, make sure to also provide a water bowl until you are certain the animals are using the water bottle. Placing the water bowl right under the water bottle spout almost ensures that your pets will bump into it, investigate, and discover that it dispenses water.

Branches or Perches

Much of a glider's exercise comes from foraging and playing in the treetops, so the cage must include various perches. Typical straight-dowel perches used for cage birds will work but are not the best choice. Natural branches or grapevines are a much better choice. Natural perches provide a variety of diameters, shapes, and textures, which enhance the exercise your gliders will receive by climbing and running along them. Make sure they are from nonpoisonous trees and have not been sprayed with insecticides. Branches should be replaced as they become soiled or shredded.

If you can get them, live fruit tree branches are excellent for your gliders' cage. Not only do they provide flexible twigs of different sizes, they enable gliders to gnaw off the bark and get to the sap. Thus, they serve as perches, treats, and even as toys, all in one—a sugar glider jungle gym with refreshments!

Toys for Your Gliders

Sugar gliders are naturally curious,

Many glider owners give their pets fabric sleeping pouches, and the gliders seem to really like them.

and they like to play with toys. If you buy toys specifically made for gliders, small rodents, or birds, they should be free of toxic paints or other hazards. It is still important to examine each toy for two specific dangers: potential nail entrapment and potential neck entrapment.

Nail Dangers

Coarse-weave fabrics and twisted-fiber ropes can catch a glider's toenail, especially if the nail is on the long side. If the nail gets snared in several fibers, it may be impossible for the animal to free itself. This can lead to injury or death as the struggling animal attempts to get loose.

Strangling Dangers

Sugar gliders can fit through extremely small openings, but manmade toys present hazards not usually encountered in the wild. A hole in a tree that is almost big enough for a glider to slip its head through will stop the animal's entrance because of the thickness of the wood, but a glider may be able to push his head through a thin ring or loop of the same size, which will then catch behind the skull, preventing the animal from pulling back out.

Make sure that any rings or loops are either big enough for the animals to go right through or so small that they can't put more than their noses through. It is surprising how small an opening a sugar glider can push his head through.

What Kind of Toys?

A glider's curiosity and explorative nature serve him well when foraging for food. He is simultaneously looking for anything edible and keeping an eye out for potential places to hide if threatened. This curiosity is the driving force behind sugar gliders' playing with toys. Objects with moving parts or those that make noise capture their interest. Larger toys that have hidey holes are also great. Since the novelty eventually wears off, it is best to provide a few toys for a while, then remove them and offer another set. By rotating them, you can keep your pets interested.

Homemade Toys

Toys for your sugar gliders are easy to make and often don't cost anything, since the materials are often otherwise thrown into the trash. Feathers, empty thread spools, corks, and many other common household items serve well as glider toys. Just make sure that anything you offer does not present any danger to your pets.

A short length of plastic chain hung from the top of the cage will be used as a swing, ladder, or trapeze. The link size should be such that the holes are not potential hazards.

Since gliders do not usually discriminate between climbing and play, replacing their perches frequently will provide them with many opportunities for exercise and fun. Branches, ropes, rocks, and vines are all suitable, and twigs with leaves or buds on them offer food treats as well as playtime.

Especially fun for a glider is a toy that contains hidden food morsels. Providing treats in this way is an important part of *enrichment—*

Clean branches and pieces of wood are suitable climbing furniture for sugar gliders.

encouraging an animal's natural behaviors. Such toys may contain compartments that open, nooks into which food items can be stuffed, or enclosures a glider can enter to find food within.

Toys do not have to be elaborate, and homemade toys are great. In fact, a favorite toy is a large feather. A feather is usually easily obtainable for free, and a glider can manipulate it, nibble on it, and shred it to his heart's content, and then you can throw it out and provide a new one. Similarly, an empty paper towel tube is often appreciated as a toy.

Wheels

Exercise is a major function of playing with toys, and most gliders love to run in an exercise wheel. However, the classic wheel composed of a circular track of closely spaced bars mounted on a wire axle should never be used for your gliders. A proper wheel will have a solid surface rather than bars so that a glider's feet cannot fall through. It will also have enclosed sides so that a limb, tail, or other body part cannot slip outside the wheel to get caught in a spoke, which can lead to injury or even death.

Your pets are naturally cautious about anything new in their environment, and it may take a while for your gliders to try out a wheel. At first, they may climb aboard, only to run off when it moves. Soon, however, they will figure it out and enjoy running.

Nesting Material

The toys section may seem a strange place to discuss nesting material, but once you've witnessed the dedication sugar gliders have for collecting, transporting, shredding, and placement of nest material, you will understand. Paper towels, leaves, grass, fabric scraps, heavy brown paper, all these and many other materials will be gathered and processed into a soft, cozy nest. In the wild, a warm, insulated nest can mean the difference between life and death, and even though your gliders will always have perfect weather inside your home, they will be just as fastidious as their wild cousins about nest building.

Friends

One of the best toys for a sugar glider is another sugar glider. Two or more gliders will race around their cage in games of tag, hide-and-seek, and follow the leader. They will spend a lot of time in joint play and then snuggle together in their nest for a nap. They

will groom each other, "talk" to each other, and keep each other occupied whenever you aren't available to interact with them. Their need for company is as comprehensive as their need for food.

Outdoors Is out of Bounds

It is never a good idea to take your sugar gliders outside in their cage. At first, you might think they would enjoy some sunshine and fresh air, but remember, gliders are nocturnal. They don't enjoy the sunshine even in the wild! Aside from temperature extremes and drafts that they are completely unused to, the outdoors

Hay, grass, cloth, and paper towels all make great nesting material.

presents them with terrifying lights, noises, movements, and smells that can easily panic them. If outdoors in a cage is such a bad idea, it's even worse to think about taking them outside without their cage!

It's a Big World

The way your gliders cling to you and quickly return to you when they go exploring can mislead you into thinking that they will act the same way outdoors. A sugar glider born and raised in captivity that suddenly finds himself outside will quite likely be completely overwhelmed. If it's daytime, the bright light will cause panic. Day or night, the alien sights, sounds, and smells will further frighten the poor animal. All of his instincts will tell him to flee, to run for the nearest tree or other vertical structure, and climb as high as he can.

The terrified glider will not necessarily stop to hear your words of encouragement or to make a mental map of where you are. From his point of view, his world has disappeared and he has been flung into a nightmarish world where nothing is familiar. He could well leap or glide from tree to tree, and in a few short moments he could be too far away for him to see you. Terrified and lost, he has little hope.

You may hear reports of bonded gliders staying with their owners when outside, peering out of a pocket to take in all the novel stimuli. There is no guarantee things will go that way, however, and even gliders used to traveling outside in a pocket can be suddenly spooked by something on a subsequent outing. Play it safe and keep your pets indoors except for trips

Natural?

Many people are confused by a distinction between natural and artificial stimuli. The nature of much animal behavior is that there is no distinction; a stimulus either elicits a behavior or it doesn't. Most animals view "artificial" or manmade habitats equivalent to natural habitats, as long as certain features are present. For example, fish and other aquatic animals will use discarded beer cans, cinder blocks, pipes, and old tires as nesting and spawning sites as readily as they will natural caves and crevices.

Several species of wild animals have larger populations and broader ranges today than they did 400 years ago because their behaviors worked as well—or better—in a human-built environment. In addition, people have eradicated large predators in most regions, giving their prey a great opportunity. Among others, raccoons, opossums, coyote, and whitetail deer are all common in suburban and urban areas. Storm sewers take the place of caves and tree cavities, garbage cans and lawns replace forests for foraging, and these animals thrive in cities using the same behaviors that serve them in wilderness habitats.

In the same way, cages and furniture can provide your gliders with all the opportunities they need for exercise and play. Your kitchen can produce fare as tasty and nutritious as that procured by wild gliders in a eucalyptus forest Down Under. A jungle gym made of dowels and ropes can elicit the same climbing and gliding behaviors as the tangle of twigs in the forest canopy does. Your kind hand and warm pockets can make your pets feel right at home.

This is why it is important to try to see things as your gliders do. When you look around, you recognize objects and surfaces according to your knowledge of things, but your gliders use their own (largely instinctive) criteria. The washing machine drain hose—glider translation: a dark, beckoning hole. A bookcase—glider translation: an easy-to-climb cliff that might have some tasty tidbit at the top. A partially open drawer—glider translation: a likely nesting spot. A television playing the news—glider translation: a warm dark hiding spot next to the wall. A visitor to your home—glider translation: another of those funny walking trees . . . maybe it has mealworms!

Gliders are perfectly capable of learning their way around their environment, whether it is an Australian forest or a living room in Manhattan. It's all natural to them, offering both dangers and delights.

to the vet, during which they should be in a secure traveling cage or carrier, not in a pocket or loose in the car.

Keeping Clean

Your sugar gliders will naturally keep themselves clean. Grooming is an important component of their individual and social behaviors. They are not, however, as fastidious about their environment. Their cage, perches, nests, sleeping pouches, and toys need to be kept clean. The nature of their diet means that their feet are often sticky with fruit juice. Coupled with

The best toy for a sugar glider is another sugar glider—or two!

their lack of table manners—they are very messy eaters—this means that their cage and everything in it or near it can get fairly messy.

Basic Cleanup

Every morning, you'll need to remove any uneaten food from the night before, wash the food bowl, and clean up any spills. Wipe down any places where you see sticky footprints. The soft, juicy foods you give your gliders will quickly spoil and create an unhealthy (and smelly) environment if they are not promptly cleaned up. If the cage has substrate, it should be replaced whenever it is soiled,

Maintenance Schedule

For cleanliness and health, stick to a regular schedule of cage maintenance.
Here is a suggested regimen:

Daily	Weekly
Change pan litter as needed.	Wash toys and provide a new set.
Empty, wash, and dry nightly food dishes.	Wash and dry cage as needed.
Rinse out water bottle and refill.	Wash and dry furnishings (perches, nests, etc.) as needed.
Check dry food dish and clean or refill as necessary.	Disinfect food bowls.
Wipe down spilled or splashed food from the cage, perches, etc.	Clean water bottle and tube with brushes, disinfect all pieces.

preferably daily. If it has a mesh bottom over a droppings tray, place newspaper or paper towels in the tray and replace them every morning.

Toys and Other Property

Sugar gliders scent mark everything in their territory, including cage parts, perches, nests, toys, food cups, etc. While it is not clear whether they also intentionally mark items in their territory with urine, they definitely cannot be housebroken, and they will leave droppings and urine everywhere. Cloth, metal, and plastic objects can be washed, while wood and rope items should be replaced as needed.

A dilute bleach solution can be used to clean cage parts, toys, and other objects. There are also a number of pet-safe disinfectant products on the market that work very well for cleaning up after your sugar gliders. When possible, dry items in the sun.

Odor Control

Are sugar gliders smelly, as some people claim? No, they aren't, but if they are not kept properly, their cages can smell bad. Any animal cage can be odoriferous if it is not cleaned regularly, regardless of the species being kept. Urine, feces, and uneaten food, if allowed to accumulate, can create nasty odors and general unhealthy conditions. Daily cleaning is the way to prevent this problem with your gliders, but there is still the issue of a sugar glider's scent.

Scent Marking

All gliders have scent glands and scent mark each other and their surroundings, but males have larger

Regularly offer your gliders new items to investigate to prevent boredom.

glands, and the dominant male in a group will do the most scent marking. Most of the time, humans cannot detect this scent, especially from a distance, but during an active breeding period it can be quite noticeable. What does it smell like?

Eau de Glider

Compared to many other mammals, human beings have a very poor sense of smell, so it is not surprising that our languages lack precise terms to describe odors. This, however, makes it very difficult to characterize the odor associated with sugar glider scent. The adjectives most often used to describe it are "fruity" and "musky," but "fruity" covers everything from a fresh-picked strawberry to a rotten cantaloupe, and "musky" describes everything from an expensive French

perfume to skunk spray. Most people do not find sugar glider scent at all offensive. If you are concerned, ask a breeder to let you smell a breeding male glider before you decide sugar gliders are for you.

Controlling the Odor

Since male gliders produce the most scent, especially during the breeding season, the vast majority of scent can be eliminated if you only keep females or neutered males. Neutered males are often available from breeders, but a knowledgeable sugar glider veterinarian can perform this minor operation if you can only find intact males.

Fruit Flies

Related to the topic of odor is the problem of an insect that can detect the odor of sugar glider food from far away—many glider owners experience a problem with fruit flies, especially in warm weather. The common fruit fly, *Drosophila melanogaster*, has been a subject in genetics labs for decades, but it is also a common pest. Leave some ripe fruit out, and they seem to materialize out of thin air. Needless to say, a sugar glider cage can be quite an attractant for these insects. They are not harmful, but they are a nuisance.

Keeping the cage and food bowls clean is the best way to prevent a problem. It is especially important to clean up any juice that is splashed around during feeding. The fermenting juice is enough to attract the bugs even in the absence of any pieces of fruit.

Toys, nest boxes, and climbing materials need to be cleaned at least weekly.

The Carrier

A small portable cage or a pet carrier will serve many purposes, from taking your gliders to the vet to keeping them safe while you clean their cage. The best have solid sides and top, with breathing holes, so that the inside is snug and dark.

Do not make the mistake of thinking that you can safely transport your gliders without a carrier just because they are so tame and bonded that they stick to you like glue. Once you're outside, they could freak out and take off. In a car, they can easily cause an accident by getting under your feet, and in a typical car, there are many dangerous dark spaces into which they can disappear.

You should acclimate your gliders to the carrier so that it is familiar and comforting, and not an additional source of stress. An easy way to do this is to include it in playtime. Put a couple of peanuts in it and leave it open. Place it open where the gliders are playing and let them scamper in and out of it. In fact, involve it in play until your pets get bored with it. Then, when you need to use it, it will be an old, familiar part of their world.

Chapter 3

Eating Well

Sugar gliders need a complete diet consisting of protein, carbohydrates, vitamins, and minerals. They have almost no need for fats, and most of their natural diet is extremely low in fat. They are insectivorous omnivores, meaning they eat both plants and animals. In the wild, they eat a variety of plant parts, including leaves, flowers, and fruits. They also catch and eat small animals, ranging from insects to small birds and mammals. As their name implies, sugar gliders have a definite sweet tooth, and wild gliders eat large quantities of tree gum, tree sap, and nectar. Understanding how they feed in the wild can help you make sense of the challenges facing you as you plan your pets' diet.

In nature, a glider's sharp front teeth are used to scrape open vines to obtain the sap.

It's a Hard Life

Studies of sugar gliders in the wild reveal that life for these little animals is precarious even at the best of times. Predation is always a concern, of course, and many gliders fall prey, but a great number also die from starvation or exposure. Especially in the more temperate areas of their natural range, a glider's ability to procure food is highly dependent on weather, being most difficult in cold, wet weather. Unfortunately, that is when energy demands on the animal are the greatest.

Coping

Small, warm-blooded animals have enormous metabolic demands—they need vast amounts of energy just to keep alive. There is a simple reason for this: The smaller an animal is, the less heat its body can retain. Heat is lost mostly through the skin, and it is generated and held by the mass of the body. The larger an animal is, the more mass it has relative to its skin—its surface area. Therefore, the larger an animal is, the smaller its heat loss over a given period of time, which translates into a smaller energy demand. Very large animals, like elephants, have a huge volume of mass compared to skin area, while pygmy shrews have a tiny volume compared to area. Elephants can easily go many days without eating and take weeks to starve to death, while a pygmy shrew must eat around the clock and will starve to death in just a few hours without food. Similarly, an elephant eats only a small percentage of its body weight per day, but the shrew eats at least 125 percent of its weight per day—more than the elephant will eat in a month!

Sugar gliders use two specific behaviors to combat their heat loss problem. The first is huddling. A colony of gliders will form one big ball in their nest, insulated by the leaves

Offer your gliders a wide variety of foods, including fruits, nuts, eggs, cottage cheese, and other items.

FAMILY-FRIENDLY TIP

I Wanna Help!

A young child can certainly watch the preparation of fresh food and help to keep the dry food bowl filled. Older children can assist in the preparation as well. Kids can also give gliders treats, but they must be instructed in how to offer the food items without the risk of being accidently bitten—they should hold the food by one end and give the other end to the glider, or hold their hand out flat with the food item in the palm.

and dry grass lining the hollow. In this way, they become a single unit thermodynamically, one with much greater mass and much lower relative surface area. The snuggled animals lose much less heat than they would individually.

The other behavior they use is called *torpor*. This is like short-term hibernation, a period of several hours during which their metabolism, heartbeat, breathing rate, and body temperature are all lowered. While it is uncommon for pet sugar gliders to enter torpor, it is very common in the wild, especially during autumn and winter, when energy demands are highest and food supplies lowest.

Gliders also cope by modifying their feeding times. Animals who are undernourished will often forage during the day, as well as at night.

Eating Well

The Difference Between Correlation and Cause

One of the most misunderstood concepts among the general public is the difference between relation and cause-and-effect. This is the reason for the popular adage *Statistics can be manipulated to prove anything*. Actually, what can be manipulated is people's minds, not the statistics.

Someone has a pain and the doctor tells him to rub glycerin on the area three times a day for a week. As the days pass, the pain goes away. The glycerin worked! No. The glycerin *may have* worked. The rubbing alone might have done it. Or, the patient might have healed on his own, independent of the treatment. Maybe focusing on the treatment made him subconsciously avoid normal activity, allowing the body time to heal. The only thing you can conclude with a fair amount of certainty is that rubbing with glycerin three times a day did not prevent healing—but it might have slowed it down. There is a correlation between the glycerin application and the healing, but there is absolutely no way to determine whether it is a cause-and-effect relationship without a great deal of further research.

What does this have to do with feeding sugar gliders? Well, very little scientific investigation has been made of glider nutrition, and glider keepers have made progress by trial and error. The problem is that when they are successful, when their animals grow well, reproduce easily, and stay healthy, it is very easy to make the connection between the diet used and the animals' condition. A breeder might swear by blueberry yogurt twice a week because once, when he didn't give blueberry yogurt, a glider got sick. The breeder observes that gliders with twice-weekly blueberry yogurt are healthy, and a glider without twice-weekly blueberry yogurt gets sick. If the breeder then concludes that this yogurt regimen keeps gliders healthy, he or she has made the mistake of confusing correlation with cause.

This may seem trivial, but if you consider the accumulation of many such instances, there is a good chance of serious confusion and misleading advice, not to mention direct contradiction. This is why it is so difficult to choose a diet from the many apparently successful ones promoted by various people. It is also the reason why so many veterinarians and breeders stress providing an extremely varied diet to your pets—it's a shotgun approach, which, in the absence of rigorous experimental data, can almost guarantee that the animals will get all the nutrients they require.

Also, since dominant animals and troupes drive subordinate gliders from prime feeding spots, the meeker animals can gain access to them by feeding while the dominant gliders are sleeping.

Rain is a special challenge, since it both makes it harder to stay warm and reduces insect activity, making it tough for gliders to meet their metabolic needs. On a rainy night, the animals may forgo normal foraging and are likely to enter torpor.

The Domesticated Advantage

Captive sugar gliders have a big advantage. They never have to deal with cold temperatures and rain. Food is always available, and they don't have to forage for it—it comes to them! It is much easier for them to meet their metabolic needs, and this is reflected in the fact that, although wild gliders frequently die from starvation, pet gliders often have the problem of obesity. Captive animals have a much easier life.

Are there any disadvantages for pet gliders in terms of nutrition? Aside from the problem we've already mentioned of getting too fat, there is a chance of malnutrition that wild animals typically do not face, and there are two reasons for this.

Unnatural Diet

Since pet gliders' food comes to them in bowls, the animals do not have the option of foraging for particular items. Wild animals naturally balance their diet by seeking out specific foods. For example, a nursing female may preferentially eat more high-protein foods to sustain her milk supply, or

Gliders who are overfed will likely become picky and eat only their favorite items.

an underweight animal might look for high-calorie items. In captivity, gliders cannot communicate such specific needs to their owners, so they get what they are served, end of story.

In addition, since the exact nutritional needs of gliders have hardly been researched, and since the exact details of their wild diet are not known, the foods we offer our sugar gliders may be deficient in some way. This is the underlying reason for the emphasis veterinarians and breeders place on an extremely varied diet. If a particular nutrient is missing in one food we offer, it may be found in a different offering. By providing a full range of foods, we greatly increase the chance of giving our pets all the nutrients they need. This, however, leads to an ironic problem—the spoiled glider.

Spoiled and Picky

All this variety makes it possible for pet gliders to get spoiled, and they sometimes pick through their food, selecting only the tastiest morsels. They may refuse to eat something not to their liking, and, worried that the gliders are starving, the owner keeps supplying alternates until he or she learns what the animals prefer. The irony lies in the fact that the wide variety of foods we offer—and the fact they we always offer plenty of food— can lead to an extremely unvaried diet when the gliders take control of things. The lesson, therefore, is that you cannot let your gliders take control! See the section "Feeding Regimen" later in this chapter for tips for staying in control of your gliders' diet.

Natural Diet

A sugar glider's diet varies from season to season and even day to day. Any wild animal has to make sure it takes in more calories than it expends looking for food. Since meals are never a sure thing for a sugar glider, it tends to eat anything edible that it comes across. Thus, we can consider a wild glider's foraging strategy to be "catch as catch can." Especially important are high-protein sources: insects, eggs, birds, rodents, etc. Any animal that can be caught, subdued, and eaten represents a nutritional bonanza for a sugar glider. Gliders aren't seed-eating squirrels—they are predatory hunters.

They Eat Other Animals?

A sugar glider's penchant for eating rodents and birds smaller than itself may not fit your idea of a cuddly pocket pet. And, while other pocket pets (like rodents) will, in fact, eat smaller animals as well, this is only an incidental part of their diet, and they are able to be kept without being fed meat. Moreover, rodents generally only eat small animals they come across, while sugar gliders will actively hunt down their prey.

In this regard, you can think of a glider as more like a cat—sweet and affectionate with people but a natural predator of small animals.

The exact best diet for sugar gliders is still the subject of some debate.

What's Best?

It may surprise you to know that people do not agree on the proper diet for a sugar glider. Different breeders are successful with different feeding regimens, and there has not been enough scientific research to answer many questions about what gliders should eat. Rodent pocket pets have long been kept as laboratory animals; their dietary needs are well understood, and there are commercial foods that can meet all their needs without the need for supplementation.

The exact proper diet for sugar gliders, however, is not known. The major controversy centers around how much protein should be fed, with some claiming that protein foods, such as milk or meat products, should make up 25 percent of the diet, while others say it should be 50 percent. Another area of disagreement is about the need for a nectar food, which is designed to replace the nectar and sweet sap of the wild glider's diet. Your best bet will be to ask the store owner or the breeder from whom you get your sugar gliders what they have been fed. Then, after consulting with your veterinarian, you can determine what type of diet you want to provide your new pets.

It is generally agreed upon that there should be three major components to your gliders' diet:

1. Protein source
2. Fruits and vegetables
3. Dry food

Proteins

Eggs, lean meat, yogurt, and live insects are all good choices for the protein part of your gliders' diet. Some experts recommend feeding

Feeding Schedule

Sugar gliders need to be fed their fresh foods every evening, when they become active. Any uneaten food should be removed the following morning. They should have clean drinking water and quality dry food (usually pellets) available at all times.

live baby mice and day-old chicks, but aside from ethical considerations, this produces a gory cleanup job. Insects fit the bill without these problems, although there are undoubtedly nutritional tradeoffs.

Eggs

You can offer your gliders eggs, either alone or blended with other foods. Cut up hard-boiled eggs or mash them with yogurt or fruit. Scrambled eggs can also be used. To provide extra calcium, some breeders put a whole egg, shell and all, into a blender, process it until the shell is completely pulverized, and then cook it.

Lean Meat

Strips of fully cooked, lean chicken or turkey are fine for your gliders. Never feed skin, bones, or raw meat.

Dairy Products

Sugar gliders should not consume milk, but cultured milk products are usually well tolerated. Milk products like low-fat or nonfat yogurt and cottage cheese are not only a good protein source, they are full of vitamins and minerals, especially calcium. Breeders often mix low- or no-fat yogurt with fruit or vegetables.

Insects

Sugar gliders, like many people, do not discriminate between insects and other small invertebrates. People use the word "bugs" to refer to any small arthropod, and gliders happily and indiscriminately consume small arthropods, including insects (like moths, beetles), arachnids (like spiders, scorpions, mites), myriapods (like millipedes, centipedes), and crustaceans (like crabs, wood lice).

It is not a good idea to feed wild-caught bugs to your gliders, as they may have been exposed to insecticides, and some might be toxic. The insects most used to feed sugar gliders are mealworms and crickets, both of which are raised and sold for use as reptile food, and both of which gliders enjoy. You should gut load these insects, which means feed them a formulation that contains protein and extra calcium before offering them to the gliders. Again, the reptile hobby enjoys many excellent commercially produced gut-load options that you can use. While crickets and mealworms are the most popular and available feeder insects, also look for sources of wax worms, silkworms, and other species.

Fruit and Vegetables

The greater the variety of fruits and vegetables that you can feed your gliders, the better. While some breeders use fresh and frozen items, others feel that fresh is best and change what they feed with seasonal availability. Nutritionally, however, frozen foods are often superior to fresh, since vitamin loss begins at harvest and continues until processing;

Eeew! Bugs!

Do you have to feed live insects to your pets? Technically, no, since you can substitute other protein sources, but gliders really enjoy live insects, and handfeeding them can be a great bonding activity. It is possible to purchase dried or canned mealworms and crickets, which might be easier for you to deal with, even if your gliders don't relish them as much.

Although feeding your gliders insects is not necessary, gliders relish them.

Eating Well

commercial frozen vegetables and fruits are usually processed within hours of harvest—long before other produce makes it to market. Avoid canned products, as much of their nutritive value is lost in processing and they often contain added salt.

Any fruit or vegetable suitable for people can be fed to sugar gliders (avoid onions, however), and individual animals have different preferences. Most gliders particularly like sweet potatoes, oranges, corn, and grapes. For the most part, they do not like bananas. You should think of these foods in terms of categories and try to include the greatest possible variety both within the groups and among them. The following ad hoc categories are not scientific and not at all comprehensive, but they should

get you thinking and serve to give you ideas of the variety you can provide.

- Berries include any berries safe for humans.

- Citrus fruits include oranges, tangerines, grapefruit, etc.

- Core fruits include apples and pears. (Remove the seeds.)

- Dark green leafy vegetables include chard, spinach, kale, collards, parsley, etc.

- Dried legumes should be fed cooked and include kidney, black, navy, pinto, butter, and lima beans; field or black-eyed peas; lentils, etc.

- Exotic fruits include figs, kiwi, mango, papaya, guava, passionfruit, dates, avocado, etc.

Dry sugar glider diets are now available, and your pets should have dry food available at all times.

- Fresh beans include green beans, lima beans, green peas, sugar peas, edamame (soy beans in pods), etc.

- Grape-like fruits include grapes of all kinds, currants, gooseberries, etc.

- Melons include cantaloupe, honeydew, Persian, Crenshaw, watermelon, etc.

- Starchy yellow vegetables include sweet potatoes, winter squash, pumpkin, carrots, etc.

- Stone fruits include cherries, peaches, plums, apricots, etc. (Remove the pits.)

- Watery-flesh vegetables include cucumbers, summer squash, tomatoes, peppers, etc.

The Expert Knows

Just Say No

Fortunately, many foods can be safely offered to your gliders, but some cannot. Common human foodstuffs that should *never* be given to your pets include:

Chocolate—toxic
Other candies—too much sugar
Fried foods—too much fat
Junk foods—too much fat and/or sugar
Onions—toxic
Artificial sweeteners—toxic

Dry Food

Dry food should be available to your pets at all times. During the day, they often wake up for a snack. The dry food offered should be the most nutritious possible, and it should preferably be made especially for sugar gliders. Dry cat food and monkey foods, which are sometimes recommended for gliders, are not at all suitable.

This is an exciting time for glider owners. The rapidly increasing popularity of these pets has created a demand for commercially prepared glider foods, and more come on the market every day. Many of the formulations include eucalyptus and other ingredients that are part of the natural diet of gliders. These are much better choices than the dry cat food, rodent blocks, or monkey biscuits that have traditionally been used for gliders. Some manufacturers offer a variety of foods, so you can alternate which dry foods you offer. Because they are dry and do not spoil, dry foods can be kept in a feeder at all times.

Other Foods

In addition to the three major types of food necessary for sugar gliders, gliders need supplements and treats. But, before discussing them, we need to look at one more natural food group.

What About the Sugar?

These animals get their common name from their sweet tooth. In fact, wild gliders are often trapped

One traditional sugar glider diet is based on honey and bee pollen.

by researchers using honey as bait. Gliders are by nature sap suckers. These animals routinely harvest sweet tree sap by biting into the bark and licking up the seepage. They eat nectar and pollen from flowers, and the flowers themselves. They nibble on the gum that exudes from acacia trees. They even eat honeydew—the sweet excretions of those insects, like aphids, that feed on sap.

Duplicating such a diet in captivity is quite difficult. A traditional recipe of honey, water, eggs, and bee pollen is known as *Leadbeater's sugar glider diet*. Some breeders offer this fresh to their gliders every day, while others use fruit as a replacement. There is no consensus about the importance of liquid foods for gliders, but we can draw a comparison to other animals: lories and lorikeets.

Lories and lorikeets are small parrots—or large parakeets—that feed naturally on nectar. For years, their dietary requirements prevented them from gaining the same popularity as pets that other parrots enjoy. Not only was a liquid diet difficult to provide and messy to work with, it also caused the birds to have extremely wet droppings, which presented significant hygienic problems. Eventually, people came up with pelleted diets for lories, and these made it much easier to maintain these birds and keep things clean.

The state of the art diet for sugar gliders is getting closer to the current status of diets for lories. Many breeders are finding that foods prepared with natural ingredients, coupled with a diet featuring easily obtainable alternatives, can keep their gliders healthy and happy without the mess of liquid diets. You should at first feed your pets the same diet they received prior to purchase, but you can gradually change them over to a different regimen based on your research and the local availability of the new commercially prepared sugar glider foods.

Supplements

Wild sugar gliders do not, of course, take vitamin and mineral supplements. They do, however, consume an enormous variety of foods that we can never hope to match in their captive

Sugar for Gliders?

Don't let the name "sugar glider" or the animal's sweet tooth mislead you. Sugar is not good for your pets. Their preference for sweet foods leads them to a proper diet in the wild, but while it will also make them eager for candy and other sweet treats, such things will only lead to obesity and malnutrition in captivity. In large part, the natural sugars in a wild glider's diet enable it to make it through lean times when very little other food is available. The recommended diet for pet gliders will provide all the natural sugars they need, and refined sugars and sweet junk foods have no place in their diet.

diet. A particular berry or bug might supply an important nutrient missing in most other foods. It is for this reason that glider breeders and veterinarians recommend that homemade diets include liquid vitamins and calcium mineral supplements. It will probably not surprise you to learn that there is disagreement among veterinarians and breeders as to how often you need to use these products, with recommendations ranging from daily to once or twice a week. Ask your veterinarian to recommend specific supplements. Generally, supplements are mixed into moist food.

Vitamins

As with other animals—including humans—the better your sugar gliders' diet, the less need for vitamin supplementation. Given enough fresh fruits and vegetables and quality protein foods, gliders will get all the vitamins they need. In the same way that some people take vitamins every day, however, some experts recommend daily vitamins for gliders. Other people focus on diet rather than supplements and stress a wholesome diet as a vitamin source. It is possible to overdose your pets and cause vitamin poisoning, so make sure that you follow the manufacturer's instructions strictly when you supplement your gliders' diet. There are many pet vitamins to choose from, and many breeders use bird or small-animal formulations, but you should check with your veterinarian.

Most breeders recommend adding supplemental calcium to a sugar glider's diet.

Calcium

Sugar gliders have specific mineral needs, and metabolic bone disease is common in pet gliders who do not receive enough calcium or who do not receive calcium in the proper proportion to phosphorus. If fed too much phosphorus, a glider cannot utilize dietary calcium. The overall amount of calcium must be greater than the overall amount of phosphorus, with the ideal being twice as much calcium as phosphorus. The fruit and vegetable diet of these animals is typically high in phosphorus and low in calcium, so many breeders supplement only calcium, in order to balance the diet. Reptile calcium supplements are popular. You can also buy a cuttlebone—the inner shell of a cuttlefish used by bird owners as a calcium supplement and beak trimmer—to use as a glider calcium supplement. Scraping the cuttlebone with a knife turns it into a fine powder that you can sprinkle over your glider's food. All calcium supplements can be mixed into food, fed to insects before giving them to the gliders, or both. Again, consult with your veterinarian.

Treats

Giving your pets treats can be rewarding, and it can be a part of the bonding process. However, treats should be part of a healthy diet, not unhealthy additions. This means that sugary and fatty foods—the kind of junk food treats that people often eat—should never be given to gliders.

Commonly used treats are bits of a favorite fruit or a mealworm. You will quickly learn what your particular gliders' favorites are, and reserving these foods to be used as treats during play time is an excellent way of bonding with your pets.

Gliders relish seeds and nuts, but the high fat content of these foods means they should be restricted to the role of occasional treats, and they should never make up a significant portion of the diet. Be aware that some uninformed sources recommend feeding gliders a parrot seed diet, but this is a horrible idea. (In fact, we now know that an all-seed diet is not good even for parrots!) Parrot seed for a glider would be like a diet of buttered potato chips for a human—extremely fattening and very unbalanced.

Food Preparation

To feed your sugar gliders, you cannot just open a container, fill the

Offer your gliders their main meal in the early evening, when they start to wake up and become active.

with spending a lot of time every evening preparing your gliders' dinner from scratch, but it isn't necessary.

Feeding Regimen

Sugar gliders begin their day at dusk, so their main meal should be offered when they wake up in the evening. Any uneaten food can be removed in the morning, after they have gone to bed for the day. By keeping a feeder or bowl of dry food available all the time, the animals can have a snack any time they want it.

How Much to Feed

A single glider will probably eat a spoonful or two of food per night. The amount will vary with the individual, with his or her particular needs (e.g., a nursing female eats more than she would when not nursing), and with the particular food. Ideally, there should be just a bit of food left in the morning, indicating that the animals had enough to eat.

food bowl, and call the job done. In fact, other than bonding time, food preparation requires the most time from a sugar glider owner. However, except for leafy vegetables, prepared food can be frozen in single-portion amounts, so you can mix up a batch, freeze it, and be set for a while. Then, every evening, you simply have to thaw a portion and add some fresh ingredients. There's nothing wrong

Eating Well

Supplements

Most breeders use a vitamin supplement, but a calcium supplement is even more important. This can be added to food, dusted on foods like mealworms, and fed to live insects right before the bugs are offered to the sugar gliders. Without sufficient calcium, gliders will develop metabolic bone disease, in which their bodies draw calcium from their bones, leading to lameness, paralysis, and death.

Likes and Dislikes

We've already discussed that it is important not to let your gliders become spoiled by giving them only what they like best. However, it is not necessary that you try to force them to eat absolutely everything you offer them. They need to eat all *kinds* of food, not every single food item. You should also realize that a glider might refuse a particular food one or more times without it meaning the animal hates that food. Often, it takes a while for gliders to try new foods. Continue to offer each type of food occasionally, over a long period of time, before you decide your gliders don't like it. Also, you may find that your gliders' preferences change over time. They may get tired of one food and begin to favor another over it.

What Do They Like?

Make sure that you evaluate each food independently. Don't always serve grapes with yogurt, for example. Your gliders might prefer the grapes plain, or the yogurt without the grapes. If you always offer sweet potatoes and broccoli, and they only eat the sweet potatoes, they might accept the broccoli when it is presented alone or with some vegetable other than sweet potatoes. It is extremely important that your gliders' likes and dislikes do not cause you to offer a skewed, unbalanced diet.

Stay in Control

A nutritional diet for sugar gliders works the same way as one for humans. If someone hates oranges but loves grapefruit, the latter will serve nutritionally the same as the former. If your gliders prefer one leafy vegetable to another, that is okay. If they don't like peas but eat lima beans, that's fine. Similar foods provide similar nutrition, so make substitutions within a group. It is important to make substitutions one at a time since, if you change more than one, there is no way of knowing what the animals' true preferences are.

The Easy Way Out

Some breeders make it impossible for their animals to pick and choose. Each day's menu includes different

Good Treats

Feeding treats is an important part of bonding. Pieces of favorite fruits and vegetables make great treats, but the absolute best are mealworms or crickets. The best way to incorporate treats into the diet is to use them as part of bonding and socializing. By reserving these special food items for this personal interaction, you increase your pets' appreciation of your time together.

Each glider will have his own individual likes and dislikes when it comes to food.

foods, and everything goes into the blender and is served as a puree. It is perfectly natural for a sugar glider to lap up a thick liquid diet, so this works very well, and supplements can also be mixed in. You will need to experiment to find what is best for you and for your gliders. People who don't like the idea of pureed foods may be reacting emotionally, from a human point of view. We would find a steady diet of food paste unacceptable, but ironically, this is what most people offer their infants. And, in fact, some glider breeders feed human baby foods to their animals. So, if it works for you and your pets, a blended diet can solve many problems and make it easy for you to stay in charge of what your gliders eat.

Clean Water

The only way to provide clean water for sugar gliders is with a water bottle. A cup or bowl will always be a mess, with urine, feces, and food splatter in it. Dehydration is very serious for a glider, and without water the animal can die as quickly as in one day. Every day, dump out any remaining water in the bottle and refill with fresh. About once a week, it's a good idea to use a bottlebrush to scrub out the water bottle. Rinse thoroughly to remove any soap or bleach residue. Having a second water bottle on hand is helpful because you can switch in the spare bottle while you clean the original bottle. Then the original bottle will be clean and ready for use next week, when it's time to clean the second bottle.

Chapter 4

Looking Good

You may be surprised to learn that pet sugar gliders do not need any special grooming to maintain their exquisite coats. You don't have to bathe them or brush their fur. Not only does a sugar glider groom itself often, mutual grooming is a significant part of their social interactions. You can still groom your pets, however, as part of your bonding interactions with them. It just isn't necessary for their appearance.

Gliders will do most of their own grooming, and they will groom each other as well.

Grooming as Bonding

Scratching and petting serve as part of the ongoing bonding process with your sugar gliders. From mutual grooming to huddling in a nest ball, many of the social activities of these animals take the form of physical contact. When a person is part of the social group, as occurs with pet gliders, the animals expect and appreciate being snuggled, cuddled, and petted. Keep in mind that your gliders will have times when they are content to snuggle and times when they want to be running around, playing. Obviously, petting is part of the former and not the latter. Having a placid glider in your lap gives you the opportunity to check on many aspects of his health. Pay close attention as you interact with your pets. By knowing how they normally look and behave, you will be able to notice any changes that might indicate a health problem.

Baths?

It is not normally necessary to bathe a sugar glider. The most common substance gliders get on their fur is the liquid from their food: fruit juice or pulp. This they will happily lick off themselves and each other. If one of your pets' fur gets especially soiled, you can generally clean him with a moist cloth. There should never be a reason to give a glider a bath, and you should not use soaps or shampoos on one. In the case of a serious soiling—with some foreign substance—the chances are good you would want to confer with your veterinarian regarding the proper recourse about the animal's exposure and condition.

Pedicures

Wild sugar gliders are forever scampering about in the forest, climbing up and down and running along branches. All this activity keeps their nails worn down, but the easy life of pet gliders often leads to overgrown nails. The more natural climbing a glider does, the less need he will have for nail trimming, so providing natural branches and logs for them to climb on will help. This is rarely enough, though, simply because of the enormous distance a wild glider has to travel during its daily foraging, as opposed to the pet glider's relatively inactive life.

Nails that are too long can cause pain and minor injury to human handlers, but much more significant is the fact that they can also get caught in nesting materials, cage parts, or toys, and this can result in serious injury or death to a sugar glider. An entangled nail can lead to the loss of the nail, a broken foot or leg, and other serious problems. It is important, then, to keep your gliders' nails properly trimmed.

Assisting Nature

Sugar glider keepers use several methods to reduce the need for nail trimming. You can provide rough rocks, such as lava rock, or even pieces of rough concrete for your pets to crawl around on. An especially nice play area can be a tower or pyramid of rocks securely glued together to provide tunnels and nooks for them to explore. Hiding treats in the tower will motivate them to explore more thoroughly. Another option is to cover one or more perches with fine sandpaper. As the gliders climb around, their nails get worn down

Grooming

While you do not need to groom your sugar gliders, they usually enjoy being brushed with a small, soft-bristled brush. They will also be very happy with petting and scratches, which resemble the mutual grooming gliders engage in naturally. Do not be surprised if your gliders groom you, too—they will probably rub themselves against you, marking you as a member of their colony.

Children's Roles

Even very small children can be taught to gently pet a glider as a parent holds the animal. Older children can let a glider climb around on them—perhaps with a treat in a pocket for the animal to find. As long as a child understands not to handle the animal roughly and not to restrain him against his will, he or she will be able to interact with a glider under parental supervision. This is a great way to foster appropriate attitudes and to educate the child to be ready to assume more responsibility in the future.

by the abrasive surface. While such measures can reduce the need for nail trimming, they typically do not eliminate it.

Clipping Nails

It is impossible to say how often your gliders will need to have their nails cut, and it is quite likely that the intervals will vary. It is not uncommon for a glider to need only certain nails trimmed due to uneven wear (probably as a result of captive life). Just keep an eye on them, and when they look long or particularly curved, trim them.

You can, of course, take your gliders to the vet to have their nails trimmed, but it is not difficult to do at home. Have your vet show you, then perhaps the next time you can do the trimming with the doctor's supervision. After that, you should be ready to tackle the job, but it still generally requires two people to safely cut a glider's nails—one to gently restrain the animal and one to do the trim. The best tool for the job is a very sharp pair of small scissors or nail or cuticle clippers. A soft cloth or a sleeping pouch can serve to restrain the glider. A glider used to being handled should not pose much of a problem.

With the animal securely held by your helper, take one paw in your hand and trim the nails, one at a time, being careful not to cut into the quick—the pink pulpy tissue down the center of the nail—which will bleed if cut. It also hurts when you cut into the quick, so expect a reaction from your pet!

The quick is usually visible in good light. Trim a small amount of the nail at a time, staying well ahead of the pink. That way, if you do go too far down the nail, you will only barely cut the quick. Some people prefer to file the nails down with an emery board. If a nail does bleed, dip it into a bit of cornstarch or touch it to a styptic pencil.

Routine Inspection

Whenever you handle or play with your gliders, you will be able to notice

Petting, scratching, and stroking your glider is most of the grooming his fur will ever need.

Healthy Ears

Sugar gliders do not usually have much trouble with their ears, but ear mites are always a possibility. These tiny parasites can occasionally be seen moving around in or near the ear, but in most cases their presence is made known by redness, itching, or crusty discharge from the ears. If you notice any of these symptoms,

anything that doesn't look right. Because of the amount of time you will be spending with your pets, you will recognize any changes in their appearance. Detecting problems early often makes it much easier to resolve them. Here are a few things you should be aware of:

Healthy Eyes

Whatever the color, a sugar glider's eyes should be clear and bright. Runny eyes or dull, white patches are a bad sign and require veterinary examination.

Providing your gliders with plenty of hard-surfaced climbing materials helps wear down claws and reduce the need for trimming.

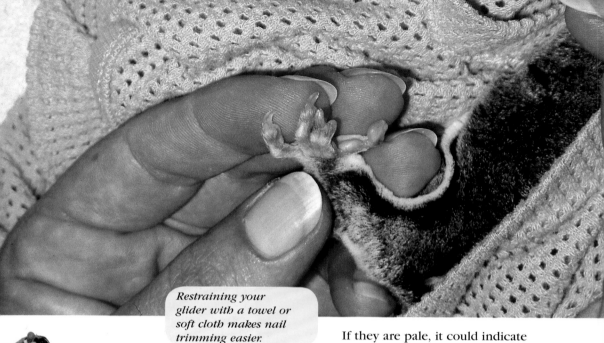

Restraining your glider with a towel or soft cloth makes nail trimming easier.

take the affected animal(s) to the vet immediately. Do *not* attempt to clean out your glider's ear! Not only could you hurt the glider, but since you will need medication in addition to cleaning, you'll have to see the vet in any case.

Healthy Noses

A glider's nose should be pink and dry. If there is discharge, or if the animal is sneezing repeatedly, take him to the vet. Gliders can catch a cold or other respiratory infection, and untreated infections can quickly get out of hand. Obviously, an occasional sneeze is not cause for concern, any more than it is for a human.

Healthy Mouths

A glider's gums should be bright pink.

If they are pale, it could indicate anemia. This is an area in which it is important for you to examine your pets regularly so that you are familiar with their normal gum color. This makes it much easier to detect pale gums.

You should also check for sores, swelling, or bumps on the gums. Very often, a gum or dental problem in an animal becomes apparent when it has difficulty eating. With an animal as small as a glider, it does not take very long at all for him to starve if he is unable to chew properly.

Healthy Fur

Beautiful and plush, a glider's fur can cover up problems, but examining it closely can reveal them. Even though your "grooming" of your sugar gliders will be more petting and scratching than brushing and combing, fur will still be your main focus. A sugar

Health Check

The time you spend playing with and petting your sugar gliders is a perfect occasion to give them an informal health exam. As you pet their heads, look closely at their eyes, nose, mouth, and ears, making sure there is nothing unusual that would indicate a possible health problem. While your pets climb around on your arms and body, check for any lameness or other behaviors that could indicate an injury or ailment. The more you know about your gliders' normal condition, the better you will be able to detect when something is amiss.

glider's fur is luxurious, soft as chinchilla fur, lush and velvety. As you hold and handle your pets, be alert for rough patches in the fur, lumps or swelling in the skin, or any other abnormality.

Sometimes, the dominant male in a group will develop oily-looking areas on his fur around the scent glands. In addition, such discolorations can turn up on the other gliders in the colony, since the dominant male will mark them often. These are perfectly normal and not in themselves a problem.

Healthy Bones

No, you can't see your glider's bones—hopefully! The early stages of bone disease, however, are often observable as a weakness in the extremities, especially the posterior limbs. Any lameness or inability to grasp is cause for concern.

An Easy Task

All in all, it is not at all difficult to keep your sugar gliders looking great. Your role is, for the most part,

simply to provide the proper living conditions, and your pets will take it from there. Some animals require a great deal of attention and care to keep their coats in fine shape, but gliders are not among them. No baths, no trims, no brushing—and yet they have a marvelously luxurious pelt! How easy is that?

The Expert Knows

Bonding

One reason sugar gliders bond so closely with their humans is that social bonding is an integral part of their nature, and grooming each other is a large part of their socialization within the colony. When you "groom" them by petting and scratching, you are not just socializing them to you, you are demonstrating that you are part of their group—just a big old glider and one of them.

Chapter 5

Feeling Good

Sugar gliders are typically hardy and healthy. Much of the task of keeping them from getting sick lies in proper husbandry. Caring for your pets properly is the best preventative. Still, like people, sugar gliders can become ill even with the best of care. Therefore, finding a veterinarian familiar with sugar glider health issues is important, and you should do this when you first acquire your pets—or even before. In this way, the doctor can examine your gliders to assure that they are healthy to begin with and can explain to you those things that you should be watchful for.

A Special Veterinarian

Most veterinarians with a small-animal practice are not accustomed to seeing sugar gliders or marsupials of any kind. In fact, a vet familiar with the treatment of these little possums is more likely to be a zoo vet. Because gliders are rising in popularity as pets, however, a growing number of veterinarians are prepared to care for them. The Internet has several glider communities that compile lists of sugar glider vets by geographical area. If you are fortunate enough to live near a veterinary college, you can probably get help there as well.

Of course, any licensed vet can supply quality care for a sugar glider in terms of general health and treatment of injuries. It is in such fields as reproduction and nutrition—places where gliders differ considerably from most pocket pets—that a specialized medical professional will be a significantly more qualified practitioner for your gliders.

Finding Your Vet

The time to locate and perhaps even meet your veterinarian is *before* you acquire your sugar gliders. There are many reasons for this.

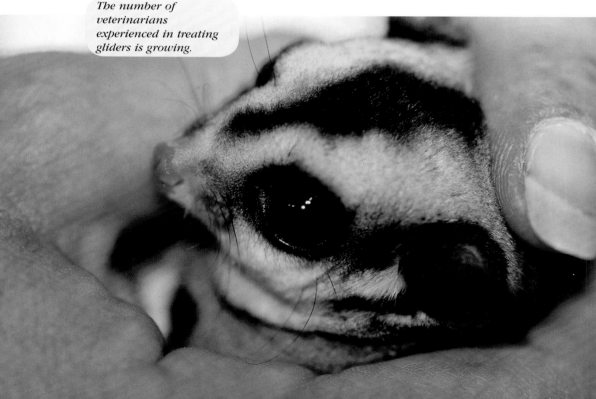

The number of veterinarians experienced in treating gliders is growing.

Security

Having a doctor all lined up before you select your pets gives you the peace of mind that this very important step has already been taken. The time to begin hunting for a glider vet is not when you have a sick or injured animal needing medical attention! In some areas, it might be quite difficult to find a veterinarian experienced in sugar glider care, and the time required to do so may be much longer than you anticipate. In the rare but not unheard of case that you cannot find a qualified practitioner within a reasonable distance, this might even cause you to change your mind about acquiring gliders—certainly, this is not something to decide once you have purchased the animals.

Help Finding Gliders

A local veterinarian who works with sugar gliders will, obviously, know people in your area who have gliders. Some of these will probably be breeders who have healthy young animals for sale. By starting with a vet, you may be able to find a source for your pets at the same time. This has the added advantage of winding up with a veterinarian who is familiar with and has been involved in the care of your pets and their parents all along. Among other things, this makes it much easier to discuss diet and nutrition, since the doctor knows how the gliders have been cared for up to the point at which you acquired them. You can also arrange to have a male glider neutered before you bring him home.

Emergencies

Accidents and emergencies are by nature unexpected, and they can happen very soon after you bring your gliders home. It's stressful enough to face injuries or illness when you have selected a veterinarian; it's much more so if you haven't. Ironically, hectic everyday life can increase the likelihood that if you do not already have a vet when you purchase your gliders, you will wait for something serious to happen before finding one. Don't procrastinate.

First Wellness Checkup

Finding a veterinarian first makes it easy to take your gliders for their first checkup right away, perhaps even on the way home with them. It is always

73

Feeling Good

It's best to establish a relationship with a veterinarian before you have an emergency.

good for the doctor to see an animal when he is well, to provide a baseline against which to compare the animal during an illness. In addition, the vet can point out any concerns with your particular pets, as well as demonstrate proper handling, nail trimming, etc.

Glider-Proofing Your Home

Unfortunately, pet sugar gliders often suffer accidental death or injury. They are extremely delicate small animals that love to investigate tiny holes and gaps, and human households typically contain many hazards for them. If you turn your back on your glider for just a few seconds, he could zip out of sight—and into a death trap.

To make things safe for your gliders, look at things the way they do. To gliders, a room doesn't contain furniture, lighting, and appliances;

it contains all sorts of fascinating objects, many of which can easily be entered through openings just of a size to squeeze through. These curious animals instinctively investigate any potential nest or hiding spot, so small access holes catch their attention much more than the objects that contain those holes. They instinctively seek out dark, enclosed areas, which means that a glider is most interested in those aspects of your home that you don't even notice, let alone focus on—areas like a gap between baseboard and floor, the space between a sofa and the floor, the area around a hose coming out of the washing machine, etc.

Let's look at some common dangers.

Mechanical Hazards

Your sugar gliders face many potential mechanical hazards. Ceiling fans are obvious ones, but a great many fans with screens or grills have openings large enough for a glider to squeeze through, thus gaining access to the whirling blades. Other devices can house moving blades enclosed in spaces with glider-size openings,

such as refrigerators, humidifiers, dehumidifiers, air conditioners, and heaters.

When checking out your home for potential hazards, don't neglect the deadly combination of moving mechanical parts and hidden, dark places. Just a few are:

- Reclining couches and chairs: Upholstery can prove irresistible to sugar gliders, and should you operate a recliner with a glider inside, you can crush the animal in the machinery.

- Garbage disposals: A curious glider who pops through the flaps into a disposal—perhaps drawn by the smell of food—is a tragedy waiting to happen.

- Appliances: In addition to those machines incorporating a fan system mentioned above, any appliance with any kind of moving parts may have openings large enough for your pets to get into, including washing machines, clothes dryers, dishwashers, and many others.

Electrical Hazards

There are two major household electrocution hazards for gliders: outlets and electrical cords. They can stick paws or noses into electrical outlets, but this is easily prevented by having all empty outlets covered with child safety plugs. The electrocution hazards posed by electrical cords are much harder to prevent and require your vigilance whenever your pets are out and about. If a curious glider

FAMILY-FRIENDLY TIP

Going to the Doctor

It is normal for a child to be a bit apprehensive when family pets are taken to the vet. Since glider wellness visits do not generally involve injections or blood tests, there should be no needle anxiety. A child who has been acclimated to regular doctor visits and explained the need for preventive medicine should not worry about taking gliders to see their doctor. In the event that an animal is sick or injured, if a child is mature enough to go to the vet with the glider, she should be able to relate this to her own visits to the pediatrician for illness or injuries. In fact, all aspects of keeping pets, including seeing the vet for problems, can be good preparation for a child in terms of being able to weather human health issues.

Supervise your glider closely when he's out of his cage to prevent him from becoming lost or injured.

decides to sample an electric cord in case it might be a tasty vine of some type, and if he chews through the insulation, it could be the last thing the animal does.

In addition, mechanical appliances are another potential electrocution hazard, since they often contain uninsulated electrical connections within an enclosed space. Even the tiniest human hands cannot reach them, but a sugar glider might very well be able to.

Toxic Hazards

Anything toxic to humans is likely toxic to sugar gliders. Most households contain a host of toxic substances such as cleaning supplies, radiator coolant, lighter fluid, paint and paint thinner, pesticides, and other chemicals. Usually, these items are locked away safely, since they represent a clear danger to life of all kinds, including that of human children. Many houseplants are also toxic— poinsettias, ivies, dumbcane, and many others—and people are generally aware of these, too.

The same is true for medications, both prescription and over-the-counter drugs. Again, most people are aware of the hazard they present and keep them out of reach. Remember that even a bottle of vitamin pills can kill. For an animal the size of a sugar glider, the lethal dose for many drugs and supplements can easily be less than one pill!

But most insidious are household items that represent only a tiny hazard to children but will quickly kill small animals. The stimulants in coffee and chocolate, which are dangerous to humans only in amounts so large they are practically never ingested, are especially toxic in rather small doses to many animals, even large dogs. Sugar gliders ingesting even very small amounts of such substances don't stand a chance.

Our veterinarian always stresses that pet animals are not little people in fur coats. Their biology is very different from ours, and not just because of size. In the case of sugar gliders, this is even more significant, since as marsupials they are biologically very distinct from human beings. Don't let your pets sample things that are not listed as appropriate foodstuffs for sugar gliders. It's not worth the risk.

Escape and Entrapment Hazards

As mentioned, the great danger is that those things that attract sugar gliders tend to be those things you will not even notice, unless you make a point of inspecting your home with your pets in mind. The place where the floor dips and forms a gap with the baseboard can give your pets access

Many houseplants and cut flowers are toxic. Keep your glider away from any plant unless you are sure it is safe.

Unplanned Pregnancies

Realistically, your sugar gliders should not be able to present you with an unplanned pregnancy. It is a simple fact that a male and female housed together will mate and produce joeys. This is why you must not keep an intact male and a female together. Your glider colony should consist of all males, all females, or females with neutered males. It is dangerous to buy a pair of young gliders and plan on having your male glider neutered before he matures sexually, since maturity is quite variable in both sexes, and some animals are very precocious. The necessary care and handling of pregnant gliders and young joeys is well beyond the scope of this book. If you do not heed the advice given here and wind up with

a pregnant pet, enlist the aid of your veterinarian, a professional glider breeder, or some other knowledgeable person regarding the necessary care for the mother and babies.

to the inside of the walls and a host of dangers, including getting lost for good. A pile of towels could easily entice a glider to burrow into it for a nap. If you grab the pile and throw it in the washer, tragedy strikes. In fact, many of your house's glider-enticing nooks and crannies pose a double hazard—first of escape or entrapment and then of a lethal hazard, including the towels in the wash, an appliance starting up, being sat or stepped upon, and a great many others. Put on "glider specs" and look around carefully. When you see a potential hazard,

eliminate it, and if you can't, make sure to keep your pets away from it.

Predator Hazards

We've already discussed the danger posed by predators that are also household pets. Dogs, cats, and ferrets are instinctively wired to view a glider as fresh meat. The other major predator hazard comes in conjunction with escape hazards. When an open space within your home gives your pets access to the outdoors, they are put into a scenario much more dangerous than wild gliders face.

Those wild animals are wary and knowledgeable, having learned the hazards they face daily from their parents and colony mates. They understand how the big world works. A pet glider has no experience and will be stunned if he finds himself outdoors. He will face a mixture of intense emotions—fear being the greatest—and he will definitely not be looking out for owls, hawks, cats, dogs, or other predators.

Dangerous Rooms

Certain types of rooms are so full of hazards that it is never a good idea to allow free sugar gliders into them. They also happen to be bad places to keep gliders in a cage.

Kitchen Hazards

Kitchens present a long list of potential glider dangers, including mechanical, electrical, drowning, burning, toxic, and entrapment hazards. While a hot stove can badly burn an unwary glider, even a cold one can harm—a furry tail brushed against a pilot light could ignite, and a glider who enters an oven vent could get lost deep inside the appliance's innards.

A glider who sneaks into an open cabinet, freezer, drawer, or oven can easily die from his curiosity. And speaking of drawers and cabinets, such areas often offer glider-size access to inside walls or crawlspaces, often places you cannot follow even if you know the glider is there.

Cooking smoke and cleaning chemical fumes can be hazardous to gliders even if they are not loose in the room. On top of all this, a kitchen is typically a busy place, often during the day, which is disturbing to sleeping gliders.

Laundry Hazards

Six major dangers for gliders come together in a laundry room: moving parts, hidden recesses, escape

While it's fun to let your gliders ride around on you, you must be careful to not take them to any unsafe areas, such as the kitchen or bathroom.

First Aid

Although you can treat small injuries on your gliders, their tiny size and fragility make it difficult to deal with much more than a superficial scratch. You should never try to handle serious injuries, and you should never try to medicate your pets except under the direction of your veterinarian. Common over-the-counter medications—even pet medications—are typically not approved for use on sugar gliders, and determining and administering the dosage for an animal that weighs 1/300th or less of the weight of a human being is impossible.

routes, drowning, electrocution, and entrapment hazards. There is simply no reason for a sugar glider to be put into a laundry room, and the opportunities for tragedy are so great that you must never make it possible for your pets to hide away in there.

Bathroom Hazards

A bathroom may or may not be an especially dangerous place for your gliders. It might be okay if you keep the toilet seat and lid down, if the space between the rim of the toilet bowl and the seat is not large enough for a glider to slip through, and if the tub and sink are stoppered and empty of water. As long as there are no openings for pipes or heating, all

windows are securely closed, and there is no space around cabinets into which the gliders can disappear, a bathroom can be a secure, small space in which you can interact safely with your gliders. Some people use such a bathroom as a "tent" for originally taming and bonding with their pets.

Stress

As in any other animal, stress in a sugar glider takes a toll on the animal's health. It also takes many forms, but it is always a reaction to some less-than-ideal parameter of the

Skunking

Like many other animals, sugar gliders have last-ditch behaviors used to deter predators once they've closed in and grabbed their prey. A panic-stricken glider can empty its anal glands, releasing a foul-smelling, vile-tasting substance that may cause a predator to drop it and flee. Called "skunking," this behavior is rarely seen in pet gliders. If you don't want to experience it, don't panic your pets!

Any change in your glider's normal behavior or appearance could be a sign of illness.

animal's environment. Very often, the result is a weakening of the glider's immune response, but other stress-related medical problems can also occur. Improper diet, disturbance of the day's sleep, and mishandling all cause a glider stress. Probably the greatest source of stress for a sugar glider is being left alone, a situation that can actually drive a glider to self-mutilation. Happy is healthy, and keeping your gliders stress-free goes a long way to preventing illness.

Disease Prevention

The best way to deal with disease is to prevent it. Often, medical problems in sugar gliders are the result of improper care and are therefore preventable. This is especially true for metabolic diseases, which are the most commonly seen medical problems in pet sugar gliders. Providing the proper diet for your pets is the best way to avoid most health issues.

Signs of Trouble

Sugar gliders, like most other small animals, don't act sick until things are quite bad. In fact, when a small animal appears ill, usually he is very close to death. After all, predators like to single out sick or injured animals, so appearing healthy is high on any small animal's priority list. Of course, when you know your pets well, you will be able to detect even small changes in appearance or behavior, giving you an early warning of trouble.

Common ailments

Sugar gliders are quite hardy and do not often become ill. In fact, injuries are much more common than diseases among pet gliders. So, preventing accidents will go a long way toward avoiding unscheduled visits to the vet.

Injuries

Being active and acrobatic, but small and fragile, sugar gliders are easily injured. Our buildings are based on the human body and pose many dangers to such small creatures. The scale of almost everything in your pets' world is way too big. Closing doors, open windows, electrical devices, even

The Expert Knows

Staying Hydrated

If a sugar glider will not drink for some reason, or if he is inadvertently left without water, he can dehydrate quickly. The major cause of dehydration, however, is diarrhea. A glider can get diarrhea from something he eats or from a pathogen—a germ that gets into his body. An animal with diarrhea can experience fatal dehydration even with a full water bottle at easy access. If a glider has two or more loose bowel movements in a row, or if its fur is soiled, indicating he has bad diarrhea, get him to the veterinarian ASAP.

the animals' cage itself can present hazards no wild glider will encounter. The instincts that serve gliders well out in the forest can often backfire and get pet gliders into trouble. If injuries occur, the services of a veterinarian will almost always be needed.

Besides accidental injuries, gliders sometimes suffer wounds from colony mates. In a bonded colony, these are a result of a temper flare or excessive mating fervor, but the wounds can be serious. They tend to be on the neck or back, in vicinity of the head. Any wound that doesn't heal right up should be looked at by your vet.

Illnesses

While sugar gliders certainly can fall ill, they are generally healthy. There is practically nothing you can do to treat your gliders for serious illness, so the important thing is to recognize when something is wrong and take the animal to his veterinarian for diagnosis and treatment.

Respiratory infections are indicated by sneezing, nasal discharge, or noisy breathing—all signals for a trip to the vet. Likewise, any unusual bleeding or discharge is cause for concern, as is diarrhea, which can kill quickly because gliders dehydrate readily. To test for dehydration, pinch the loose skin at the back of the neck into a tent, then release. If the skin immediately

Gut loading your glider's insects with calcium-rich food will help prevent metabolic bone disease.

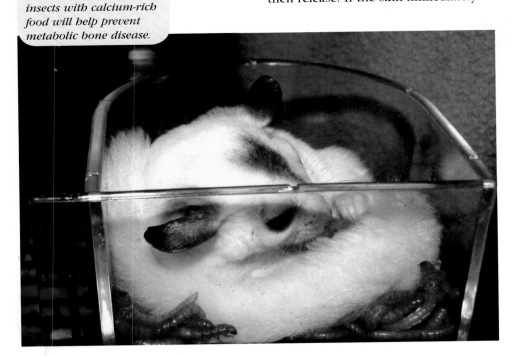

A glider who is kept by himself will be lonely and prone to problematic behaviors.

returns to normal, the animal is properly hydrated; if the tent remains or flattens only very slowly, the animal is in danger of death and needs immediate emergency rehydration at the vet's.

Metabolic Disease

Metabolic bone disease is unfortunately common in pet gliders. It is a condition caused by hypocalcemia, or low levels of dissolved calcium in the blood, and therefore in the body. We discussed this in Chapter 3, in conjunction with diet and the required balance between calcium and phosphorus, since a glider can develop hypocalcemia even in the presence of sufficient calcium

if he eats an excess of phosphorus. The fruits and vegetables we feed our gliders tend to be simultaneously high in phosphorus and low in calcium— the reverse of ideal. This matter has not been well researched, but it is likely that the wild sugar glider's diet is balanced mostly by the consumption of other animals. Insects are the most common live foods given to pet gliders, but most insects are low in calcium, too. The consumption of birds, reptiles, and small mammals is certainly a major source of calcium for wild sugar gliders. For many people, however, providing these is not an option. This is where calcium supplements come in. When you discuss your gliders' diet with your

Remember to include provisions for your gliders in your family's emergency plans.

Emergency Preparations

Since emergencies by definition are unplanned, having ready-made plans prepared on a contingency basis makes a lot of sense, and it could make the difference between life and death for your gliders. At the very least, you should have a secure carrier on hand in which your pets can be safely carried, either in the case of a general emergency, like a natural disaster, or in case they need to see the vet. It's a good idea to keep a container of your gliders' dry food with the carrier. If you are forced to flee your home, your pets can survive for a while on that. Include a spare water bottle.

veterinarian, she can recommend how to use these supplements.

The symptoms of calcium deficiency are typically lameness and hind-leg paralysis. By the time you notice the symptoms, the disease is well advanced, and immediate medical intervention is required to save the animal's life. If you notice *any* weakness in a glider's limbs or a reduced ability to grasp with hands or feet, get your pet to the doctor as quickly as possible. Metabolic disease can be treated, but it can also be quickly fatal. Therapy at the first sign of weakness provides a much better prognosis than if you wait for paralysis to set in.

Parasites

All mammals can suffer from parasites, both external, like fleas, lice, and mites, and internal, like intestinal

Wild-caught insects sometimes carry parasites. It's safest to feed your gliders store-bought bugs.

worms. Do not use anti-parasitic treatments intended for other species on your gliders. If you detect or suspect parasites, bring your pets to their vet as soon as possible. The doctor may require a stool sample from the animals to check for worms. Remember to check their ears regularly for unusual discharge or other signs of ear mites. Make sure you follow the instructions carefully when dosing or treating your pets, and don't use medications prepared for other types of pets, except under a veterinarian's supervision.

How Did He Catch *That*?

Pet owners whose animals never go outside are often surprised when their pets get fleas or worms. After all, they didn't have any contact with wild animals, so how can they be infected? While being completely indoor pets protects sugar gliders from many sources of infection, there are still ways that they can come in contact with parasites or their eggs.

Obviously, if you have other pets that go outdoors (even if only on a leash), those animals can bring the problem in with them. You can also unknowingly transport tiny bugs or eggs on your shoes and clothes. Some insect pests can enter your home on their own, through open windows, gaps around doors, or other openings.

Parasites are not a major threat to your indoor gliders, but you must be attentive. If you fail to catch them early, a severe infestation is likely.

Psychosocial Problems

Psychological problems? No, you aren't going to need a sugar glider therapist, but it is important to be aware of the importance of social contact in your pets' health. This need is very strong, but it is also very simple. Sugar gliders must have company, period. A lone glider is a sick glider. The symptoms of the sickness cover the entire spectrum and can vary from anorexia (not eating) and starvation to obesity from overeating, from pining and wasting away to self-mutilation.

You already know not to purchase a single glider, but what do you do if death leaves you with one animal? In such a case, gliders almost always will accept a new companion, although it is important to acquaint the two animals slowly, as described in Chapter 1. Remember that even a very lonely sugar glider will see a new glider as an invader of its territory, so give your solo glider plenty of time to adjust to the newcomer.

Smelling Good

We've already discussed preventing odors by daily cleaning, and we've talked about the natural scent marking these animals do. Sometimes, however, gliders—or rather, their urine—can smell very bad. In most cases, this is a result of an unbalanced diet or of overdosed supplements. Consider it an early warning sign of something wrong, and find out what part of your pets' diet needs to be remedied.

Feeling Good

Chapter 6

Being Good

While many small mammals make wonderful, affectionate pets, in the wild their greatest concern is avoiding predators. Most predators are considerably smaller than a human being, which means that we must really appear monstrous to the poor little animals.

Fortunately, it is quite easy to get past their instinctive fear, simply by handling them. When a sugar glider is handled by people from the time he leaves his mother's pouch, he accepts humans as nonthreatening. In fact, he comes to see a person as a great big friend, and he is happy to seek the protection of your hand, or even your pocket! He also quickly learns to associate you with food, which strengthens the bond.

It's possible that tame sugar gliders think of their people mostly as warm, friendly trees, as large bodies with lots of dark pockets and sleeves to hide in and producing tasty treats on occasion. In any case, once bonded, your gliders will be happy climbing all over your clothes and head. They will also glide to your hand or arm from the top of curtains, bookshelves, and the like. A bit disconcerting is the habit some gliders develop of coming in for a landing spread-eagled on their owner's face! Such bizarre "hugs" are not painful, but many people prefer offering an arm for a landing spot.

Handling

The proper way to handle sugar gliders is often and gently. Even a well-socialized animal will demonstrate initial nervousness with a new owner. Patience is required to get him to bond with you. If he was not tame to begin with, bonding will require a great deal of patience. Be calm and consistent, and your pet will come to trust and love you.

Starting Out

It is a good idea to leave your gliders alone together for a couple of days when you first get them. Give them time to adjust to the sights, smells, and sounds of their new home. Many people recommend placing an article of your clothing or something else you have worn or handled into their cage to convey your scent. Gliders recognize others through smell, and if your smell is associated with their nest and home, you will be familiar to them. If they are willing, feed them treats through the bars or wire. Once they've settled in, reach into the cage to stroke them. Move very slowly so you don't startle them or make them feel chased. If they

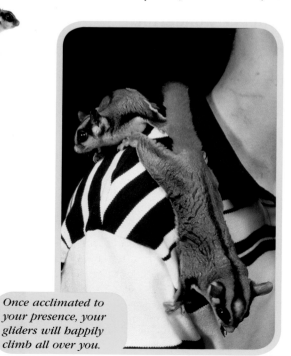

Once acclimated to your presence, your gliders will happily climb all over you.

FAMILY-FRIENDLY TIP

Children and Gliders

Because sugar gliders are small and fragile, they must be handled with extreme care. Even a child's strength is more than sufficient to injure or crush a glider. A toddler's hand can be guided to pet a glider gently. Older kids can pet a glider or offer him a treat. As they gain responsibility, children can hold a glider—with adult supervision. Make sure that you always demonstrate proper handling so that your children will appreciate the correct way to interact with their pets. The absolute dedication of gliders to their people makes them as interactive as a loving puppy or kitten, and children will delight in playing with them, but the gliders' relatively small size means that extra caution is required.

start crabbing or acting nervous, back off. Try offering a mealworm or other treat. The first few times, just leave your hand in place after they take the food. After that, try to pet them. Remember, patience is the keyword. Well-socialized young gliders may in fact react to you by jumping onto your hand and climbing to a pocket, but if they don't, just keep at it.

Daily Handling

While you will definitely enjoy your time with your gliders, for them it will be the highlight of their evening. If having a sugar glider climbing all over you, running up your sleeves, and fishing for treats in your pockets doesn't sound like fun, then perhaps a gerbil would be a better choice for a pet. Gliders are true "Velcro pets," and although they will career around the room, as well as all over you, they will often be back for a quick snuggle before resuming their antics.

Basic Behaviors

Pets generally have to learn to *behave*, to learn certain rules of behavior to fit in with their human families, but sugar gliders are not that kind of household pet. You cannot housebreak them. You cannot train them to come when called, or to sit or lie down, or to stay off the drapes. You cannot train them not to crab or bark. Nevertheless, you can *shape* their behavior. If you call their names or make a certain noise every time you feed them, they might—if they feel like it—come when you signal them. By placing treats at certain spots in the room every time you let them out, you can teach them to take a certain route. Use only positive reinforcement; in other words, do not yell at or punish a glider if it does something you don't like. Instead, reward him with a treat when he behaves the way you want.

Potty Training

It makes sense that many people want

to potty train their sugar gliders, since they are so much fun to carry around in a pocket or sleeve. Unfortunately, it also makes sense that these animals are not really potty trainable. A wild sugar glider may never touch the ground during its entire life. They are inhabitants of the forest canopy and live among the branches and leaves, often at a considerable height. Animals in this environment simply pass their wastes—literally into thin air. Burrowing animals, on the other hand, live in close quarters and very often instinctively use a designated toilet area, or at least do not soil their living areas.

Sugar gliders will pee and poop wherever they are when the urge hits—in their cage, in a sleeping pouch, in your pocket, down your sleeve, on the drapes, on the floor. They are less likely to soil their

sleeping area, but they are by no means consistent in that. Some owners report success in getting their gliders to cooperate by indicating when they need to go, but don't count on this working with every glider.

Biting

The mouth of a sugar glider holds many more teeth than a human's—about a dozen more. These teeth are used to slice through tree bark and to kill and devour a large variety of animals. Obviously, the bite of a sugar glider is, despite the small size of the animal, not a pleasant thing to experience on your finger. On the other hand, it is hardly life-threatening, and you must not react as if it is.

Sugar gliders only bite in self-defense, and it is possible for you to threaten them without realizing it.

Crabbing is an early warning signal that a glider is getting annoyed or feeling threatened. Grabbing a sleeping glider is a good way to get bitten, and any glider who is hurt or feels cornered may bite. Since early socialization is the best way to tame a sugar glider and to overcome any fear of humans, it is also the best way to avoid defensive biting. If a glider is not afraid, he won't bite.

It is very important not to react badly if you are bitten. Realize that biting is a last-ditch, extreme measure for a glider, a defensive one elicited by fear or pain. Here is an instance when you must suppress your own instincts. Many gliders are hurt or killed when a human flings them across the room in a knee-jerk reaction to dislodge them from a bitten finger. The proper reaction is to gently disengage the glider (though they rarely hang on) and then discover what caused the bite and make sure you correct the situation. Care for the bite as you would any other small wound: Clean it and the surrounding area and bandage it if necessary.

Can I Train My Gliders?

Sugar gliders generally do not learn tricks. They are intelligent and able to learn a lot of things, and you can use positive reinforcement to shape certain behaviors, but do not expect your pets to perform like a trained dog—sit, stay, roll over, etc. That said, sugar gliders have learned some very complex behaviors simply by having each little step rewarded as it is learned.

Treats and Training

Treats used in training have to be very small since, once the animal is full, treats will no longer have an effect. If your gliders have a favorite fruit or vegetable, small bits of the food can serve as treats. Food items like sunflower seeds or peanuts that should not be part of the regular diet are good for treats as well. In fact, reserving such treats for training is a great way both to limit how much your gliders get and to keep them extra special (and, therefore, keep your gliders motivation to learn the trick high).

The trick is to start by building on a foundation of natural behaviors—running, climbing, jumping, even gliding. Set the goal as a long combination of little behaviors that, when strung together, produce the effect you want.

If you want to build a course that includes straight runs, trapezes, rope swings, and leaps over gaps, you can probably train your pets to run the course, provided that you break it up into a string of single, small behaviors

FAMILY—FRIENDLY TIP

Children and Training

While young children should only play with sugar gliders under your supervision, older children are sometimes perfect trainers. Kids can have a great deal of patience with animals and are delighted with every step of progress. Often, the bond between a glider and a young person is greater than it is with adults, who are easily distracted and less intensely focused on the animal. And while you may not really care much about your gliders' "performances," a child can find them very significant and worth a lot of effort.

that can be rewarded incrementally until the whole course is learned. It will take time, but it can be done.

Patience and repetition are the keys. Make sure the glider knows one step perfectly before you add the next, at which point you should stop rewarding the first step and offer a treat when the animal begins the next desired behavior. Gradually require more of the desired behavior before giving a treat. Once the new behavior is learned and the animal can perform the two in sequence, move on to the third step. In this way, you can build up quite complex behavior patterns.

Socialization

Getting your gliders accustomed to interacting with people and other animals is called *socialization*. While socialization to humans is the foundation for sugar gliders bonding to their owners, socialization to other animals can lead to problems.

Humans

For the most part, a sugar glider's socialization to humans should be started long before he is placed in a home. Breeders typically begin the process shortly after the joeys leave the pouch and continue it while they are in the nest. By the time they start venturing out of the nest, the joeys will already be tame and affectionate toward people.

Animals who are socialized early in life will be calm and friendly with family members, friends, and visitors. In a real sense, this involves their learning that it is not simply the humans to which they are bonded who are safe, but all people. Well-socialized gliders will still need to bond with you, however. (See "Bonding," later in this chapter.)

Other Animals

In the natural state, sugar gliders interact with four types of animals, so let's examine how each type will affect the pet glider.

Other Sugar Gliders

Other sugar gliders are either colony mates or interlopers. The first are recognized by the colony scent and are accepted completely; the latter are recognized by the lack of colony scent and are driven off—violently if necessary.

Smaller Animals

Almost all animals that are smaller than sugar gliders are considered prey and will be killed and eaten. This includes insects, spiders, and other invertebrates, as well as small birds, reptiles, and rodents.

Similar Animals

Animals of similar size and habits will probably be seen as competitors by gliders and driven away. If they are not seen as competitors, they will probably be ignored. For domesticated gliders, this means that they may or may not get

Teach your child to handle your gliders gently and calmly.

OOP?

In many ways, the point at which a sugar glider joey leaves his mother's pouch and begins to live in the colony's nest is equivalent to the birth of a placental mammal. The joey is still not completely developed, is still dependent on adults for its care, and is just beginning to learn about life outside of Mom. This is why the age of a sugar glider is usually given in time OOP—time out of pouch. The ideal age at which to get a glider is when it is a couple of months OOP.

along with other pocket pets. There is a good chance that gliders will see them as meals, however. No matter what, your gliders should never be left unattended with other small animals.

Larger Animals

Sugar gliders interpret larger animals as predators for the most part. Fleeing from large herbivores is a mistake they can easily afford to make if they also flee from all large carnivores! Partly taking their cue from you, your pets may learn not to fear the family dog or cat. This is not necessarily a good

A Language Lesson

The word *anthropomorphizing* refers to projecting human attributes onto nonhumans. We are all guilty of it when dealing with our pets, and it is certainly true to some extent that many animals have human-like traits. It is dangerous, however, to get carried away to the point of thinking that a companion animal is a little furry person. It is impossible to know in any animal—including humans— what its thoughts and feelings are. The only way we can read such things is by interpreting behaviors, and this is often a very unreliable method. Translating behaviors into thoughts and emotions is fraught with difficulties and pitfalls. You are "translating" sugar glider into human, without the aid of a dictionary.

In fact, translating between languages can give us insight into this problem. Two common problems are relevant to the issue of translating a pet's behavior. The first is mistranslation due to false assumption. Often, a word or a phrase in one language will sound a lot like a word or a phrase in another language. This can lead to direct misinterpretation, as it did for a college friend of mine and his classmates. They were learning Indonesian from a native speaker, and were doing drills from the book, going around the room, each person taking the next item. After each response, the teacher would say, "Very good," and the next student would take a turn. It was a few days before they discovered that the instructor was not praising their wonderful performance. He was saying "berikut," which means "next" in Indonesian! A nonlinguistic example would be the forced "grin" often seen on trained chimpanzees' faces; this is an expression of fear, not amusement. Or, as we discuss in this book, interpreting a dog sleeping with a couple of sugar gliders cuddled up next to it as meaning the dog loves the little marsupials, when it could very well be that the dog has simply learned to tolerate them and is glad they are worn out and ready to nap.

The second common translation problem deals with what linguists call "false friends." These are words in one language that seem to be the same as in another language—but aren't. There are long lists of these language pitfalls, many of which produce humorous or awkward situations, but which can also seriously derail negotiations. A well-known example is found with French and English:

French *attendre* means "to wait for," not "to attend."

French *assister* means "to attend," not "to assist."

An interesting animal example is found in a mother hen's behavior. Watching her care for her chicks, constantly checking them and fussing over them, can easily lead you to think she has human-like maternal feelings toward them, that she loves them. Everything she does confirms your interpretation of love. If you place one of the chicks on the other side of a fence, the mother will try desperately to get through the fence to her frantically chirping baby. However, if you slip a glass jar over the chick, so that the mother can still see it but not hear it, she will walk away from the fence and the chick. The bird has an instinctive response to the sounds the chick makes, and when those sounds are obscured, there is no more response. However disturbing, it is a natural behavior, hardwired into the animal. It is extremely difficult to believe this when you see so many behaviors that support the idea that she loves her chicks, but it is necessary to conclude that if chickens love their babies, it is a very different sort of love than what humans feel.

Make sure that you keep these things in mind. While you may understand your pets' behaviors, you may also grossly misjudge them. It is completely unfair to base your expectations of your pets on *your* understanding of their thinking and emotions. If your cat kills one of your gliders, it didn't violate a sacred concept of family—it simply acted naturally, and you completely misunderstood its prior behavior toward the glider.

thing because these larger animals can hurt or kill a sugar glider without even meaning to do so. One misplaced paw is all it would take.

Family Pets

First, cats and dogs can easily harm or kill a sugar glider in play. You may think the dog "loves the gliders as family members," but the dog may think they are really cool, animated plush toys. And even if your dog *did* see them as family (translation: pack) members, he could still easily injure them in trying to get them to play. This isn't the worst, however.

All animals, even the dog, which has been domesticated for many millennia, retain natural instincts. Dogs and cats are predators, meat eaters with very specific hunting skills. These instincts can remain latent for a long time, until a certain stimulus elicits an automatic behavioral response. It is important to realize that we are not talking here about thoughtful or even intentional actions. A cat who feels like hunting may go to an area where it knows mice live and start inspecting it, but a flash of movement of a certain type can evoke an attack in a cat

who is just strolling across the living room. The cat's eyes and brain are wired to perceive certain movements and to respond immediately, without thinking, planning, or intention.

Many glider owners will proudly show you photos of their pets riding on their dog's back or eating out of a bowl with the family cat. Yes, it is possible for both the glider and the dog or cat to coexist with the other animal. They may get along perfectly,

Once bonded to the members of your family, your glider will consider them to be part of his colony.

Getting Lost

There is always the chance that your gliders will get lost. If you have a good lock on the cage and never leave them unattended when they are out of the cage, you will minimize this chance, but it can still happen. Very often, a lost glider has simply slipped from view and into a hiding spot. However, the longer a glider is unaccounted for, the less likely it is that you will be able to recover him.

This is a case where bonding proves to be quite advantageous. A glider who is bonded to you, who looks to you as the provider of food, who loves being handled by you, will return to you readily. Talk to the unseen animal, get out a favorite treat that he can smell, and if only one of your gliders is lost, put his cagemate(s) into a carrier next to you. They may do the job for you and call the delinquent back. Once everyone is home safe, fix things so that the same escape cannot happen again.

but they have not actually learned to accept the other animal as family. The tragic thing here is that what the glider has learned—thanks to your intervention—is that the dog or cat is safe, when it isn't. The dog or cat has learned simply not to be annoyed by the little creature. One day, the glider may move or enter the dog or cat's visual field in a certain way, and in less than the blink of an eye, the glider is dead. Sometimes it never happens. Sometimes it does. It simply isn't worth taking the chance.

Bonding

Socialization makes a young glider comfortable around humans, but bonding is what happens when gliders make you part of their family. A tame animal is not afraid of you, but an animal bonded to you loves spending time with you, snuggling with you, playing with you. It will accept you as one of its colony mates—albeit a rather strange one!

It is astounding how close this bond can be, especially given our immense relative size. How comfortable do you think you could be with a 2-ton (900-kilo), 75-foot (22-meter) tall creature handling you? While gliders are quite content to treat a human as a jungle gym or tree trunk, it is clear that they demonstrate affection toward their owners as well, enjoying a warm cuddle by their human as much as a high-speed game of tag up, down, and all around their friend's body.

Leashes?

The subject of walking a sugar glider on a leash is highly controversial. You will find specially designed glider

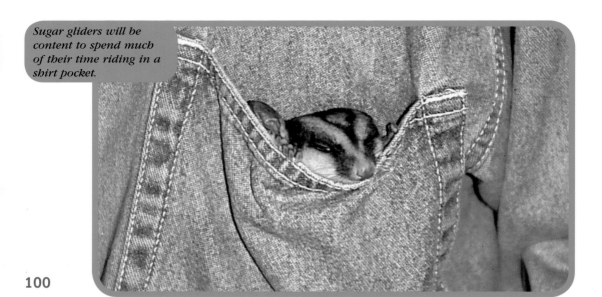

Sugar gliders will be content to spend much of their time riding in a shirt pocket.

harness and leashes for sale. Some people promote their use and point out that a leashed glider is safer than one running loose. This argument, however, fails on two counts.

Tragic Accidents

For a harness to stay on a sugar glider, it has to fit rather snugly around the animal's neck and/or chest. Because gliders are small and delicate, with fragile bones, such restraints are quite likely to injure or kill them. Since the whole point of a leash is to restrict the animal's movements, to physically hold him back and pull him in another direction from the one in which he is heading, it very likely risks strangulation or broken bones. To make matters worse, those who promote leashes often advise keeping them on even when you are not on the other end—leashes make it easier to retrieve gliders and to keep an eye on their location, they argue. This, however, is a terrible idea.

Impaired Rescues

Leaving aside the argument that a glider trailing a leash is like a person dragging around a heavy chain that weighs a substantial percentage of his or her weight, a glider so tethered is at a greatly increased risk of getting stuck somewhere. Gliders are pretty good at judging spaces they can just fit into, but they don't take into account a harness and leash. They may be unable to turn around or to back out of a confined space because of the leash, and, since a leash is harder and stronger than a glider, when you try to extricate the poor animal, you may inadvertently crush it.

The Greatest Tragedy

Most tragic of all is a determined little sugar glider, who, encumbered by a leash and unaware that his owner has gone to answer the phone, struggles to climb to the top of a chair, then launches into the air to glide to the couch. The leash loops around the chair, and the glider snaps to a sudden halt. The owner returns to find the beloved pet dead, hanging by its neck. Hopefully, this image will convince you not to try to turn your gliders into poodles. Leashes are for dogs, not possums!

Combat

Sugar gliders are, for the most part, gentle and peaceful. They are, however, capable of aggression. Unlike some animals, like wolves, gliders do not have elaborate behaviors to indicate submission. This is because aggression is typically shown only to gliders from other colonies, and the losers of these territorial disputes simply run away. In captivity, fights can be bloody and deadly because the loser doesn't—can't—run away, so the attack continues.

Infrequently, two gliders in the same colony may squabble. Occasionally, a wounded animal will result, usually one with lacerations on or near the head. The severity of the wound will determine if the glider needs veterinary attention. Minor cuts can be kept clean and watched for signs of infection. If a wound needs stitching, your vet will probably discuss the use of a collar to prevent the glider from reaching the wound and pulling out the stitches.

Fun and Games

Usually, the only "bad" behavior your pets will engage in is mischievousness, and perhaps an obsessive need to check every square inch of your clothing for hidden treats. Overall, sugar gliders are free of vices—unless you consider excessive *joie de vivre* a vice!

In the wild, these animals use their skills and cunning to find food and avoid predators. In captivity, where those two concerns are eliminated, they can direct their time, energy, and intelligence to play. And they are more than happy to include you in that play. If you are willing and able to provide the necessary care, these beautiful and clever little animals will gladly make you friend and family. Exotic marsupials, sugar gliders are wonderful companions and can be your friends for a great many years.

Glossary

albino: a sugar glider that lacks melanin, resulting in a white animal with pink eyes

arboreal: dwelling in trees

Australasia: the region including Australia, New Guinea, Tasmania, the Bismark Archipelago, and many nearby islands

barking: a yelp gliders use to express excitement or alarm or to keep in contact with other colony members

crabbing: a grinding sound gliders use to express displeasure

domestication: process of selectively breeding an animal over generations to live in close association with humans usually as a pet or work animal

exotic animal: any animal that has not been domesticated, even if the animal is tamed and socialized to life with people

joey: unweaned baby glider

marsupial: a mammal that gives birth to premature young, which reside in the mother's pouch until mature enough to survive in the outside world

marsupium: the fur-lined pocket or pouch in which the young of female marsupials nurse and grow

melanin: dark-colored pigment found in the skin of animals

patagium: the extensible fold of skin between a glider's front and hind limbs that allows him to glide

***Petaurus breviceps*:** scientific name of the sugar glider; it means, roughly, "short-headed rope walker"

pocket pet: any small mammal kept as a pet, including hamsters, gerbils, mice, rats, guinea pigs, and sugar gliders

wild-type: a normally colored sugar glider

Resources

Rescue and Adoption Organizations

Lucky Glider Rescue and Sanctuary
Phone: (903) 482-6026
Fax: (877) 738-7099
E-mail: rescue@LuckyGlider.org
www.luckyglider.org/

Petfinder
www.petfinder.com

Rattie Ratz: Rescue, Resource, and Referral
2995 Woodside Road
Suite 400, PMB 325
Woodside, CA 94062
Phone: (650) 960-6994
www.rattieratz.com

Although focused on rats, this organization rescues other small mammals too.

Small Animal Rescue Society of BC
PO Box 54564
7155 Kingsway
Burnaby, BC V5E 4J6 Canada
Phone: 604-438-4366
Fax: 604-777-2118
www.smallanimalrescue.org

SouthEast Sugar Gliders Rescue and Sanctuary
www.southeastsugargliders.org/

Suggie Savers
www.suggiesavers.org/index.html

Wee Companions Animal Adoption, Inc.
San Diego, CA
(619) 934-6007
www.weecompanions.com

Internet Resources

The Glider Initiative
www.thegliderinitiative.org/

GliderCentral
www.glidercentral.net/ubbthreads/ubbthreads.php

Gliderman's Sugar Glider Page
//gliderman.tripod.com/index.html

Gliderpedia
www.sugarglider.com/gliderpedia/index.asp?TitleIndex#preview

The Gliding Room
www.sugarglider63.com/faqs.html

North American Sugar Glider Association
\\mynasga.org

Pocket Pets Online Community
www.sugargliderinfo.org

Ruth's Sugar Glider Page
www.sugarglider.com/archives/ruth/

SugarGlider.com
www.sugarglider.com

Sugar Glider Care
www.sugarglidercare.net

Sugar Glider Care.org
www.sugarglidercare.org

Suz' Sugar Gliders
www.suzsugargliders.com/

Publications

Magazines

Fur and Feather
Elder House
Chattisham
Ipswich
Suffolk
IP8 3QE
United Kingdom
01473 652789
info@furandfeather.co.uk
www.furandfeather.co.uk

Books

Fox, Sue. *The Guide to Owning a Sugar Glider*. TFH Publications, Inc.

O'Reilly, Helen. *A New Owner's Guide to Sugar Gliders*. TFH Publications, Inc.

Veterinary Resources

Association of Exotic Mammal Veterinarians
www.aemv.org/vetlist.cfm
This site lists exotic mammal veterinarians by location.

Association of Sugar Glider Veterinarians
www.asgv.org

Index

Note: Boldfaced numbers indicate
illustrations; an italic t indicates tables.

Index

About the Author

David E. Boruchowitz is foremost an "animal person." He has been keeping and raising animals his entire life. He has extensive experience caring for fish, herps, birds, and mammals, and he has shared his life with many small mammal pocket pets. Believing that knowledge is the key to forging a bond of friendship with our pets, he has dedicated his professional life to educating people on how to understand and care for their companion animals. He has written dozens of animal care books and served as Editor-in-Chief of *Tropical Fish Hobbyist* magazine.

Photo Credits